"An insightful manual written by an authority in this field."

—*Author's ex*

\*

"I really wish I wasn't dating her. I'm probably going to marry her just because I'm afraid of what might happen if I call it off."

—*Author's boyfriend*

\*

"She learned from the best. This book really pulls together generations of knowledge from the biggest lady-squawkers I've ever known."

—*Author's grandfather*

\*

"I couldn't put it down. I'm thrilled to know there are other women out there just like me."

—*L. Bobbit*

# I Used to Miss Him . . .
## But My Aim Is Improving

*Not Your Ordinary Breakup Survival Guide*

Alison James

Adams Media
Avon, Massachusetts

*To women everywhere:*
*May your exes cause you only a fraction of the pain that you cause them.*

Published by
Adams Media, an F+W Publications Company
57 Littlefield Street, Avon, MA 02322. U.S.A.
*www.adamsmedia.com*

ISBN: 1-59337-011-3

Printed in the United States of America.

J I H G F E D C B

**Library of Congress Cataloging-in-Publication Data**
James, Alison.
I used to miss him, but my aim is improving / Alison James.
p.    cm.
ISBN 1-59337-011-3
1. Man-woman relationships. 2. Interpersonal relations.
3. Interpersonal communication. I. Title.
HQ801.J278 2004
646.7'7—dc22
2003022942

Cover illustration by Mike Lary.

*This book is available at quantity discounts for bulk purchases.*
*For information, call 1-800-872-5627.*

# Acknowledgments

*I would like to thank* everyone who has worked so hard to put this book together, particularly Danielle Chiotti, my editor, for her patience, enthusiasm, and tireless effort; Paul S. Levine, the fastest agent in the West, for giving me a go and selling like a fiend. I would also like to extend my gratitude to everyone at Adams Media, the men who put on their girly caps to understand this idea, and the women who convinced them not to run for their lives.

Special thanks to my parents, Shirley and Joseph Hovancik, and my two sisters, Vanessa Shuba and Tina Reno, for surrounding me with plenty of humor always. There are so many other people who have been very helpful and made contributions to this project, particularly: Sarah McDaniel, Kate Brame, Colette Curran, Liz Leo, and Tom McDonough—thanks, guys! Special thanks to Art Vomvas for keeping bankers' hours. And last but not least, my love and gratitude go out to Thomas J. Howe for his endless encouragement, support, and sense of humor.

Heaven has no rage like love to hatred turned,
Nor hell a fury like a woman scorned.

—William Congreve, *The Mourning Bride*,
1697, act III, scene 8

# Table of Contents

# Introduction

Nothing about breaking up with someone is easy, especially when you feel like you're getting the crappy end of the deal. In fact, going through a breakup is arguably one of the most miserable experiences in life, akin to having an arm gnawed off by a large, rabid dog or getting your pant leg stuck in a moving truck when you're biking. It's painful, it comes out of nowhere, and it just plain sucks.

But before you let any guy twist your heart into a knot and pull it out through your nose, remember that every horrible breakup has a bright side. Things really could be worse. At least you didn't stay with him, only to find out years later that he has a lengthy criminal record or the need to experiment with his sexuality. It could happen. It's happened to the best of us. But it is admittedly hard to have such intelligent perspective at the time of a breakup. It is much easier to focus on the fact that the guy is gone (not to be mistaken for "goner"—that comes later).

So you wonder what you did wrong, analyze his words and actions, critique your own hair and clothes, and measure yourself against other girls. Or maybe you try to find the one thing you did that drove him away. All the while, a lump in your stomach grows and you contemplate trying to suffocate it with chocolate fudge sundaes. The pain is a constant distraction. You find yourself taking your pajama bottoms to the dry cleaner or letting the iron burn a hole through the board. Your mind is always somewhere else, dealing with the shock of losing him. You finally decide that if you can just find a large quilt and cut a space in it where someone can shove food in with a spoon, you can feasibly hide in bed for the rest of your life.

Then someone calls, your sister or a friend, and says, "Come on now. You'll get over him. He wasn't right for you anyway." Then another chipper person follows up with, "You are so pretty and smart. Clearly, there's something wrong with him." You feel better temporarily and think, "They're right. I am far too good for the major-loser scumbag." Then, alone at night in your room, your emotions swing the other way and your tears return for an encore. Day after day, week after week, you love him, then hate him. You want him back, then want to kill him. Your emotions take you on an up-and-down roller coaster ride—off the track, onto the fairgrounds, and right over the wires holding up his Ferris wheel car. Woops. Rides are so dangerous.

The Greek goddess Hormonia now rules your days. You start to feel like an emotional nut job, even though in reality you're just going through the standard breakup fare—shock, tears, rage, and the urge to pull a few saucy maneuvers. Maybe you want to call your ex at 3 A.M. and then hang up on him, have friends from out of town prank him so he can't trace the call back to you, or wait outside his apartment in an obscure location to see if he is going on dates with other girls. Maybe you feel a little more creative, so you think about writing him venomous notes or e-mails spilling out your feelings. Or perhaps you simply want to dump the poor guy's brand-new container of orange juice down the sink the next time he's sick. As mild as these gestures are, you still can't help but think, "Maybe I do go a little bit overboard at times. Maybe I'm psycho after all."

Interestingly, you aren't. You have no plans to hurt him when he's in the shower. That definitely means something. Clearly, he's the maniac wearing the hockey mask and carrying the ax. And it looks like he twirled that sucker around a bit, lost control, and took off the top part of his hair. Hence, the big bald spot.

The reality is that there are astounding similarities in the post-breakup behavior of all sassy divas, and therefore your reactions are perfectly normal. Any girl in her right mind would chuck a beer in a guy's face if he deserved it, or read his e-mail if he had a history of lying. Who wouldn't put a guy's shorts through the paper shredder, or hitch a train to his summerhouse at 2 A.M. to tell him off? We're not crazy. We are simply . . . hmm . . . well . . . spirited and energetic. It makes perfect sense. After all, we're a generation of smart, sassy, confident women and we do things our way. When we feel emotional, vulnerable, or insecure, we might crawl into bed and eat Ben & Jerry's for a few minutes, but then we jump right back out and say, "Watch out jackass. You've been a jerk and I'm not going to let you get away without a little bit of suffering." Then, if there's any B&J's left, we put it back in the fridge for later (behind the ice cube trays so no one else eats it) and get to work.

The feeling of personal power that comes from dreaming and scheming is liberating, and it helps us get back on our feet again. It is not something we should be ashamed of, but instead is a comical sign of how resilient and spunky we truly are. We no longer play by the rules; we make our own. Of course, we still feel hurt by a breakup, but we aren't pathetic or broken. Our spirit becomes even stronger and more defiant when challenged by a difficult man.

*I Used to Miss Him . . .* is a breakup survival guide that recognizes and celebrates this resilient spirit in us all. Combining practical advice with a "Rip the bastard's head off" twist, these tips and suggestions will help you forget about him and take back your life. Unlike traditional breakup advice that teaches you ways you can fix yourself, this handy manual provides a comprehensive plan that will help you fix his ass, too.

So gear up, read on, and get ready to dazzle the world with newfound dash. The era of the sassy chick has come and it's here to stay. She's confident. She's daring and she's spunkier than ever. And you will be, too.

## Chapter One
# Face the End with Courage

Like a hike through a rain forest full of creepy exotic bugs, the end of any relationship is full of surprises sure to make you jump a mile and scream "eeeww." The things he says and the thoughts that pop into your head can leave you confused and certain the earth is crumbling beneath you. During these final moments you might feel an overwhelming urge to cry and let it all hang out.

But as a sassy diva, your new mission is to let nothing hang out—except your arrows if they don't fit into your cute handbag just so. Get through the finale with class and poise and save your most emotional side to show your avid supporters later in the privacy of your own pad. Face the end with courage and attitude and arise from this finale a triumphant diva with a martini (and maybe his credit card) in hand.

## Signs Along the Finish Line

*How could this be happening? What changed?* These are the first questions that come to mind when he brings up the end, and they get the emotional waves rolling. One minute he's planning a trip for two to the Caribbean, and then suddenly he needs time to himself. He's busy at work. He's going out of town. You can't believe your ears. He's either had a brain transplant or he's lost his mind.

Guys have a special gift for ambiguity. Maybe it's because they grow up using sign language on the baseball field and basketball court. They never seem to learn that taking a girl out to dinner, buying her a rose, and then not calling for four days is not a clear way to communicate one's level of interest. So don't beat yourself up if you didn't see the breakup coming. It's definitely not your fault, and you have every right to be upset and annoyed.

Identifying the signs of an impending breakup is not easy. And while you may have missed some major clues this time around, there's no reason that it should ever happen again. So take some time now to identify the end-of-the line signs that rolled off your ex's body like nasty post-workout sweat. Following is a list of common clues that the end is near. Read it over and see if any of these things resonate with you. Copy it and hang it on your refrigerator. Commit it to memory. Pass it out to all of your girlfriends. It will help ease some of the shock right now—and armed with your new ability to read caveman code, you'll be able to make the pre-emptive strike next time.

Give your ex the benefit of the doubt. He might think he dropped a hint when he stopped signing his e-mails "love." It's very possible his self-awareness does not expand beyond his e-mail signature.

Sassy Scoop

## End-of-the-Line Signs

If several of these statements ring true, the guy could be getting ready to initiate a breakup. Actually, the word "initiate" makes him sound proactive—in reality, he will probably grunt the news after he leaves you crying on a street corner.

* He drinks beer all day and watches sports events with his feet propped up. (Okay, just kidding about that one!)
* Normally he would e-mail you ten times in a twenty-four-hour period. Lately he only writes once or twice a day, and each message is shorter than usual. Spam is pouring in, so you know your account is working just fine.
* When you talk to him on the phone, he is always distracted. You hear video games, a radio, or a nose-hair trimmer in the background.
* He picks fights over how you squeeze your toothpaste, accuses you of stealing the remote, and turns up the volume on his television when you're trying to tell him a story.
* You find yourself wishing you were back with the guy you dated before him, the one who has since realized he's gay and loves fake fur.
* When you ask him if there's any milk left he yells, "Stop pressuring me."
* He says things like, "Why do girls care about weddings? Do they just want some stupid piece of crap on their finger?"
* He has no interest in participating in activities with your friends or family. He can't remember your best friend's name, and she's his sister.
* He is suddenly obsessed with work. You haven't seen him in weeks except for the day you met him in the office cafeteria for a nutrition bar.

* He doesn't help you when you need it. You call to tell him your refrigerator stopped working and he suggests you hang your food outside the window in a laundry bag.

* He criticizes your clothes, your hair, and how you talk. He asks you why you can't be sexy like _____ (insert Hollywood's flavor of the week). He talks excessively about another girl—someone he works with, someone he knows from college, or a friend of a friend.

* He simply stops paying attention to you, even when you are together. You pull up in front of his house on a Harley sporting a blue mohawk and wearing a saran-wrap dress and he doesn't even flinch.

* He stops planning dates, trips, holidays, anniversaries, and weekends. If he has time to plan for the Super Bowl and not for your Saturday night date, you have a problem on your hands.

* You call him and he says, "Oh. Hi, Jen." Your name is not Jen.

* He remembers and repeats lines from every movie he ever saw, including the scintillating dialogue from his midget porn tape, but he forgets your birthday.

* Stories of men leaving their wives remind you of him and make you wonder what he'll be like when he's older.

* He's disrespectful. He shows up late. He forgets to call. He always puts his friends first. He doesn't listen to you when you talk. He doesn't take you seriously. He belittles your dreams or goals.

> If you do break up with him and he truly loves you, he will shape up quickly and try to win you back. In this case, the power is yours and you can demand a massage every night for the rest of your life.
>
> Sassy Scoop

Whether or not a breakup is pending, a man is not properly worshiping you if he's doing several of the things on this list. It is up to you to decide if you can live with his behavior. Maybe he is normally Prince Charming and his flagrant actions are an anomaly. If you think he might change, hang in there and wait it out for a bit, but be prepared because he might not change at all. He might break up with you or, worse yet, he might keep you in his life at arm's length so you never feel loved and appreciated. In this case, chopping off his arm is an option, but you might want to go with something that's less likely to result in large legal fees that you could otherwise spend on a new wardrobe.

If you're not happy, the gutsiest option is to get out of this relationship and start over. It may be a hassle, but it is more of a hassle to deal with a flawed jerk for the rest of your life. End-of-the-line signs are glaring messages from the Goddess of Divadom. She wants you to do the right thing no matter how hard it is to do, and the right thing is to call it quits when the guy you're dating is not giving you the love and respect you deserve. So when you get the feeling in your gut that something's not right, listen to it. Your intuition won't help you win the lottery, but it will tune you into his intentions and prevent you from experiencing a lot of unnecessary heartache.

> If you think no end-of-the-line signs existed in your most recent relationship, look harder. Inevitably, they were there, buried underneath your ex's smelly socks.
>
> **Sassy Scoop**

*I think; therefore I'm single.*

—*Lizz Winstead*

## Quiz  Are You the Queen of Rationalization?

Do you ignore end-of-the-line signs at all costs and come up with reasons why they aren't that big of a deal? If so, you might be the Queen of Rationalization. It is important to recognize your tendency to rationalize things and stop doing it so you don't end up with a guy who treats you poorly. Take this quiz to help you determine how close you are to being crowned Queen.

1.  He never calls you back. You say:
    a.  Damn bastard. To hell with him. I hope he gets the phone cord caught around his neck.
    b.  He hasn't been calling? Oh, I didn't even realize it. I've been on a trip with _____ (insert name of hot guy).
    c.  I forget to call him sometimes, too. Maybe he thinks I don't like him. Maybe I need to try harder to show him how much I care.

*If you picked "c," slap yourself on the wrist and call a diva who picked "b" to find out if her traveling partner has a cute friend.*

2.  He didn't invite you to his friend's wedding. You think:
    a.  I have to act fast if I'm going to sneak in and put a bug in his salad.
    b.  He hates to dance and I love to. He probably thought I wouldn't have a good time with him.
    c.  I hope he enjoyed the day because he'll never have his own wedding if I have anything to do with it.

*If you chose "b," scold yourself for a few minutes. Then, put on a great dress, turn up the music, and dance your way down to the local bar to meet a new guy.*

3. He never offers to pay for anything. You think:
   a. How cute. The poor guy must be saving cash to take me on a trip to Paris.
   b. He's a selfish ass who buys nasty no-name-brand toothpaste at the dollar store.
   c. Either he makes up for being a penny-pinching pr*ck with one piece of jewelry equivalent in price to all the crap I've bought for him or he is history.

   *If you picked "a," give yourself a kick and then get rid of the pr*ck. Buy yourself a plane ticket, fly to Paris on your own, and dine with a suave Euro-stud.*

4. He has been acting strange. You think:
   a. I'd better run before I find out he's being featured on *America's Most Wanted.*
   b. I've been insanely bitchy due to PMS, so it's probably my fault.
   c. Unless he's had a death in the family, he has twenty-four hours to clean up his act or he's out of here.

   *If you picked "b," take a Midol, grab a scepter, and crown yourself Queen. Then refer to "c" for the real answer.*

5. He told you to lose weight and made fun of your new haircut. You say:
   a. You look like you're wearing an inner tube under your T-shirt. At least my padding is in the right places.
   b. Excuse me? Did you just dare to insult me? You'd better sleep with your eyes open, buddy, because I will cement your mouth shut if you make one more comment like that.

c. He's right. I've been letting myself fall apart lately and he always looks so good. I'd better work harder on my body.

*If you selected "c," you need a serious infusion of diva sass. Thank Mr. Loser for imparting his useful observations, and then leave him behind to find his perfect plastic princess.*

If he does one thing wrong now and then, it's okay to let it slide. However, if you find that you are constantly making up excuses to justify his behavior, it is time to put your foot down and insist that he treat you the way you deserve to be treated. If he decides to leave instead of change, so be it. How much rationalization are you willing to do before you tell him you're tired of his poor behavior? Ask yourself that question when you find you're spending too much time making excuses for his lame-ass ways.

## Off-Again, On-Again?

If you are certain it is over with your ex (so certain that you've ironed your black veil and buried his pictures), you can skip this section, but if there is even a slight chance that this breakup is just one of the small tremors preceding the big quake, read on. Like a

### Kill Him with Kindness

A guy of the jellyfish variety will try to get you to break up with him by being a jackass. Subvert his plan by performing your "sweet as pie" act. When he's annoying, be as kind as possible and tell him you love him—with honey dripping from every word. Eventually he'll give up on his spineless plan and talk.

stubborn stray eyebrow hair, every time you tweeze him away, the bastard's back, and it's crucial that you know how to handle him.

Apart-together-apart-together, your relationship is starting to remind you of gym-class calisthenics. When you are apart, you both field 4 A.M. phone calls from each other and make drunken promises to be "different." When you are together, you spend your time in Discuss the Relationship (DTR) mode, trying to live up to those promises. You keep your end of the deal, becoming June Cleaver for a stint. In turn,

Trust your inner guidance system. When that little voice in the back of your head tells you to kick his ass, go for it.

Sassy Scoop

he no longer drinks directly out of your milk carton and he calls if he's going to be two hours late. You're excited. You're making progress. "It's only a phone call," your friends say, "he should be doing that anyway." But you know he's really trying this time. These calls are a big deal for him, and you try to convince your friends that he has a new attitude, with new and improved excuses. He's had a horrible case of phone-phobia since he was two because his mother—the cruel wench—used to leave the ringer on next to his crib. Explanations roll off your tongue until one day they turn to curse words and you're back at square one. Then the whole process begins again.

To survive a breakup successfully, you have to be committed to the idea that the relationship is definitely over for good, that all the signs and symptoms of disaster are there for you to heed. Recovering requires a great deal of energy and enthusiasm. If some part of your mind is still thinking, "Things aren't so bad. We might get back together," you will not have the enthusiasm it takes to put your spunky foot forward and move on.

If you are having trouble steering clear of the "I know we're going to get back together" trap—or if you broke up, but now he's sidestepping toward your door again and you don't know whether to leave it open or slam it when he's halfway through— commit to memory "The Sassy Rules for Getting Back Together with an Ex," and follow them with conviction.

### The Sassy Rules

\* If he initiated the breakup, or acted like a monster for a long time so *you* would, then he must say explicitly that he would like to give the relationship another try. He must do so in a responsible, respectful way, asking forgiveness of the goddess he almost lost.

\* If he has been calling you, or you are mutually sobbing to each other, then let him into your life, slowly, armed with a sharp utensil in case something goes wrong. Remain cautious.

\* If you haven't heard from him in weeks and suddenly he's knocking on your door at 2 A.M., yelling your name like Rocky in round ten, fasten the deadbolt, go back to bed, and wait to see if he comes back when he sobers up. A blubbering, inaudible yell does not qualify as responsible or respectful.

### A Sassy Battle Plan

If he's crying and begging but you feel like he's still too much of a bastard to deserve a second chance, take him back for just a day or two and implement one of these tactics to fix him good:

- Secure embarrassing photos of him to use in the future.
- Tape soaps over his favorite movies.

- Refill his bottle of regular ibuprofen with nighttime pain relief tablets.
- Buy him a few ugly shirts to wear out and tell him they are totally sexy.

The bottom line—make sure you only take him back for the right reasons, and that you think about it first. If he initiated the breakup, he is uncertain about the relationship in some way, however small, and you cannot do anything to change that. Being nicer won't change it. Being more available won't change it. Doing little things for him, calling him, begging him, pleading with him, and so on— none of these actions will make his confusion go away. It's possible that someday he will become certain you are "the one," but he has to decide that on his own. The sassy diva that you are doesn't have time to wait around for his revelation. If you are available when it happens, that's great. Until then, live your life without him in it and have a fabulous time. You will never be happy if you commit 100 percent of your energy to a guy who only gives you 50 percent in return.

If your dog gnawed your finger off, you'd be careful around him for a while before you nuzzled into his fur again. Just like your barking buddy, your ex needs to be approached with caution. Unfortunately you can't restrain him with an electric fence, so you will have to use your own devices, notably prudence, common sense, and an automatic weapon strapped firmly to your waist.

Sassy Scoop

## The Big Finale

You've broken up and gotten back together a dozen times and you've rationalized his every move to death, but in the end you decide you just can't make excuses for this dead-end relationship any longer. It's just plain over. You know in your heart that you will never be with this person again. These final moments are difficult, but you are a diva. You will survive the finale and arise strong, confident, and ready to move on.

The relationship finale can take many forms, all equally difficult to handle. The end might be a huge screaming match or a simple acknowledgment of the problems at hand. It could be laden with phrases like "this isn't working for me anymore," or "guess what? I'm moving to a new city" or nothing more than the garbled words "I want to date other people."

> Never sleep with an ex thinking it will bring you closer together. If he gives you a diamond necklace, you can consider it—but make it only a fleeting thought, and only after you've had the necklace appraised.
>
> Sassy Scoop

Regardless of what the ending is like for you, you are not alone. Emotional, dramatic, and even wacky responses to a breakup are universally par for the course. Most likely, your experience was a variation on one (maybe more) of the following categories.

### *"But you said you would love me forever?"*

The soft, loving, and trusting approach. You really believed in him and he broke your heart. You're not mad (yet)—you just want to know why he's breaking up with you. You still love him as much as you did yesterday, so you can't snap your fingers and turn it off just like that. How did he?

You remember all the sweet times you had together and review again and again his kind words. He said "I love you" and he even talked about the two of you moving to a tropical island together. So how come now he never wants to see you again? Was it all an act? It doesn't make sense.

Disbelief quickly turns into a feeling of sudden loss, which in turn leads to a crying binge. Once you move into this mode, there is no turning back. The tears come forth like a monsoon and your sense of shame vanishes. You find yourself lying on the floor grabbing onto his leg when he tries to leave. Men should be happy about this, because a "female leg attachment" actually makes them much more interesting than they could ever hope to be on their own.

### "You're a jerk. How can you do this to me?"

The dissed diva approach. You're the spirited type, which means that his speech will provoke rage instead of tears. You spew forth the "F" word in a silvery symphony. You pick up his CDs and crack them in two, catalog his every flaw and blame him for world hunger. In the heat of the moment, you rip up his photo and throw it to the ground. You jump up and down on the pieces and shout, "Die, scumbag, die," as he backs toward the door. To you, this opportunity to see him cower is just one of many perks of breaking up. An hour later, the whole thing really hits you. You think about it and become enraged again. Then your mind shifts to something more important—have your theatrics given you the most dreaded female label of them all—psycho? When you walk into an interview in five years, will your new employer pull out a file that says "nut job"? Don't worry at all. "Psycho" is just a guy's way of labeling you so he doesn't have to feel guilty about how badly he treated you. Know this: You are not psycho. Besides, even if you were, you could still have an amazing political career.

*"Okay. That's cool. See ya around. What the hell just happened?"*

The totally indifferent approach. Before he begins to speak, you know something's wrong, but you remain calm and act natural. When he finally lays it on, you feel your face turn red and your heartbeat accelerate, but you blame your watery eyes on allergies and cheerfully grab a tissue. Once he's finished talking, your response is limited to something as simple as "Oh, okay. It's not exactly what I want, but I understand where you're coming from. It's probably for the best." You maintain a calm, cool tone of voice and apathetic facial expression with every word you speak. Then, even though your heart is twisting into a knot, you hold it together until he gets out the door. As soon as he's a block away, you call your best friend and cry your eyes out.

*"Excuse me . . . uh . . . are we breaking up?"*

The "it would be nice if you told me what the f#@!ck is going on" approach. You get back from a week-long vacation and there are no messages from him. You call him and get his voice mail. He doesn't call you back. Finally, concerned that he's been abducted or is trapped under the free weights at the gym, you contact his friend to find out what is going on. His roommate tells you, "Um, look, I think he just wants to take a break, ya know." "What?" you ask. "And that's how he plans to tell me?" You decide to go wait outside his door, but instead you find a way in. You make yourself at home in his kitchen, baseball bat in hand, and wait for the thug to return.

*"No way. I was the one who was supposed to break up with you."*

The slighted approach. You didn't even like him at first. He seemed awkward and a little bit nerdy. Now he's breaking up with you? You look at him in utter disbelief and you want to scream, "You are the lesser social being, the one I never even wanted to go out with in the first place." But you can't say it because he's been accusing you of acting disinterested for months and you aren't going to give him the satisfaction of knowing he was right. You feel annoyed and even upset. You start to cry and suddenly you look at him and think . . . maybe he is "the one" after all. He seems cuter in a way and more appealing now that he's being an ass. It's as if his words alone have transformed him into the superstud of the century. You're aware that it is a bit twisted, but you don't care. You're hurt and you want him back.

## The Emotional Storm

Though every breakup is different, they all share common elements: a bastard ex, a hellish finale, and a subsequent whirlwind of emotions that mix together to form a breakup hurricane. Once your ex is out of sight, you'll find yourself raging with fury one minute and then feeling overwhelmed with sadness the next. Or you'll start obsessing about his every move and then have the urge to tie his arms behind his back and slap him silly. These reactions are not signs that you are losing your mind. In fact, they are signs that you are quite normal and sane. It would be crazier if you didn't feel like you were living through the hurricane of the century.

Become familiar with these emotions now because even though they start during the finale, they stick around long after it's over to annoy you while you're coping. They are like little mosquitoes that take turns biting you. The good news is that being aware of them is the first step toward squashing them.

## Maddening Moods

You've probably exhibited one (or all) of these moods as you go through a breakup. Relax. They're kind of like the five states of breakup grief. They're perfectly normal, and they won't last forever.

### Confusion

You ask yourself questions like, "Where did I go wrong? Will I get through this?" You don't know how it happened. You think you have amnesia or dementia or one of those brain diseases.

### Hurt

You feel lonely and even defeated. You just want to bawl your eyes out. It seems like the more it all sinks in, the more difficult it is to deal with. You can't move from the spot where you're lying down because you might puke. Your stomach feels worse than the most horrendous hangover you've ever had.

### Obsession

Every little thing reminds you of him. He liked iced tea, so you can't drink it. He slept on your favorite pillow, so you get sick every time you look at it. The toe of one of his socks is sticking out from under your bed and you feel like it's mocking you. The rest of your life has stopped, and nothing matters except coping with the ordeal.

Delusion

Your ex momentarily becomes the perfect god of studliness, unparalleled by any other man alive. Your mind erases all the annoying and nasty things he did, and you convince yourself that you cannot live without him.

Anger

You look at yourself and realize you are a damn attractive, smart, and fun person. How dare he do this to you? He makes you so mad you want to tell him off. In fact, you want to scream at him from the top of a building through a bullhorn. He doesn't deserve to be happy again for the rest of his life. You resolve that he won't be if you have anything to do with it.

These strong emotions will wax and wane in an unpredictable fashion, making you feel as if your mind is swerving all over the place. But they don't have to send you careening down the breakup highway from hell. Just buckle up, regain control, and be prepared for the emotional ups and downs that lie ahead. You can't keep yourself from having these breakup feelings but you can recognize that they are normal. Then step on the gas and whiz by them toward a happier place.

**Timing Is Everything**
If you have to make a major decision and it happens to fall right around the breakup, try to put it off for at least a week. Though it might seem appealing, now is not the time to commit to relocating to the African jungle.

## The Crime Scene

If there's one element that can turn mere breakup discomfort into surgery without anesthesia, it is location, location, location. If a breakup at your own place is difficult, a breakup in the car, on vacation, or in any unusual venue is pure torture. With a little preparation, you don't have to be caught off-guard while backpacking on a snowy ice cap or slogging through the desert. You can avoid precarious places—or at least know what to do if you find yourself breaking up in one.

### *The Vacation Split*

You're away with him at a tropical resort. Something seemed wrong on the plane ride there. He wouldn't stop staring at the flight attendant with perma-smile. So you're not surprised when he breaks the news over fu-fu drinks on the boardwalk. Why did he bother following through with the trip? And more important, what the heck are you going to do for six days, upset, angry, and miles from home?

Very few divas opt to stick it out on a trip that begins with a breakup. But if you have the will to do it, move to a phenomenal room at another beachside resort and make him pick up the tab. If you just want to get out of that godforsaken place, stick him with the airfare home. This whole mess is his fault, so make him pay for it.

If the two of you are on the rocks when you get there, the most likely possibility is that you'll suffer through the week in limbo and then break up on the way home midair. Look at the bright side: you do have airline drinks, and soon you'll be back in a place where you have the home court advantage. Until then, have some fun. Make the most of the fact that you have the little slug trapped in a flying tube high above the ocean:

- Let the flight attendant know about his "special" meal request.
- Ask the slow-speaking old woman about her grandchildren.
- Encourage the baby behind you to cry.
- Let your carryon belongings make their way over onto his lap.
- "Accidentally" spill the remainder of your red wine on him.
- Sniffle twice per minute throughout the entire flight.

### The Public Scene

A breakup in public usually draws a fair share of curious onlookers as well as couples who are glad they aren't the attraction this time. You're crying and trying to face inward toward a wall so no one can see what's going on, but both of you keep raising your voices and blowing your cover. Eventually you opt to talk through your teeth, and then you can't understand each other. So you throw caution to the wind and turn the whole thing into an all-out screaming match. When you realize people are watching, you just want to crawl under a rock and die.

Don't let a public scene get you down. If you're in a mall or around people you will never see again, the aftermath won't be quite as bad as you think. If you are at a big party with friends, they will feel slightly relieved that their dumb, drunken actions are overshadowed by the drama. In either case, you can make this situation work in your favor if you call upon your sass. Simply fabricate a few false lines about your ex, yell them aloud, and let the rumors begin:

✱ I am so tired of catching you wearing my bras and underwear. I don't know what your issue is, but you need to deal with it fast.

✱   Look, buddy, this whole crush thing on _____ (enter most obnoxious guy at the party's name) is not only weird for me but for everyone in your life. If you're gay, just say it. No one is going to like you less if you admit it.

✱   I don't know whether or not you should go for the enlargements. Nothing you do down there is going to improve things for me anyway.

Your ex might retaliate with a worse fabrication, but people will be so busy spreading the news that they won't even hear his attempted retorts.

### Holiday Hell

Preholiday breakups are among the most dreaded kind. They always seem to happen at one of those Norman Rockwell Christmas parties where everyone's singing carols and drinking eggnog. Then suddenly you're boyfriend-less and surrounded by couples exchanging gifts. The holidays are always a tough time for newly single divas as the commercial fanfare moves in for the emotional kill. But don't let impending holidays make the relationship seem more important than it really is. You can take control of the situation and enjoy the season even more with the bastard gone.

**Gift-Giving Secrets**
If things turn sour around the holidays or his birthday, make sure any gift you buy for him is appropriate for your father, brother, or male friend. You don't want to end up stuck with the pink bow tie he wanted.

You can also have a little fun with festive traditions. Send him a helpful gift that reflects your opinion of him—maybe a helpful sex tips book, weight loss magazine, or home vasectomy kit. Swing by his place to sing a few carols with friends. Stand outside his door with a dozen or more divas and sing aloud a special holiday song:

Oh ~~Christmas Tree~~ Mini-Wee
Oh Mini-Wee, Oh Mini-Wee, You have a tiny willy;
Oh Mini-Wee, Oh Mini Wee, I want to slap you silly.
As time has passed, I hate you more;
Your new girl is a little whor . . . bore.
Oh Mini-Wee, Oh Mini-Wee, You have a tiny willy.

Or try any of these other holiday breakup favorites:

- *Away in a ~~Manger~~ Prison*
- *We Wish You a ~~Merry~~ Wretched Christmas*
- *~~Rudolph the Red-Nosed Reindeer~~* _____ (insert ex's name) *the Big-Nosed Jackass*
- *The Twelve Days of ~~Christmas~~ Paybacks*

Maybe you'll make the holiday section of your local paper for spreading good cheer across your community. And don't forget, holiday parties are full of new guys to flirt with under the mistletoe.

## The Workday Nightmare

The phone rings five minutes before your big meeting and you think it's going to be the annoying guy from accounting asking you about an invoice. It's an annoying guy all right—the one who's calling to break up with you at the most inopportune time. You hang up the phone after the deed is done, and you have thirty seconds to get to the conference room to give your presentation.

Hopefully the shock is strong enough to numb you for a few hours until you get through your marathon meeting. If not, the other voices in the room should lull you into hypnosis for a while. There is only one way to deal with a workplace disaster, and that's to feign illness and leave while you can. So contract a momentary fit of flu, throw up all over the place, and get the hell out of there. There's no time to waste on spreadsheets and memos. You need to start putting together a sassy battle plan immediately.

### Calling off the Wedding

If you are dating a man that is bastard enough to break up with you before your wedding, you are a special diva deserving of an extra-long, extra-sharp arrow to hurl his way. How dare he show up at the church and yell "stop" in the middle of the ceremony and then break up with you right in front of your groom-to-be? What nerve!

If he *is* the groom, he is jackass undeserving of the air he breathes.

A prewedding split must be taken with a pinch more seriousness than the average breakup. If you have invited a hundred guests, picked out everything from flowers to a honeymoon package, and talked about the wedding until visions of church bells rang in your head, you are going to feel tempted to keep the jackass around and give it another try. However, no level of groveling describable in words will make up for his big, huge, gigantic mistake. Basically, the only excuse that's even remotely acceptable is the plea of temporary insanity, backed by several

**Commitment Phobia?**

Tell any guy you're dating to "sh*t or get off the pot" if too much time passes without a commitment. Though you are never to blame for a guy's actions, you must take responsibility for what happens if you allow him to linger on forever without proposing to you. If you don't want to marry him, that's a different story. But if you have marriage in mind and he is not doing something to get things moving down that path, walk.

notarized certificates from psychiatrists around the world. If he cannot provide these documents promptly, you have no choice but to do away with him for good.

Start by sending follow-up cards to your guests saying "The Wedding Is Off. The Groom's a Bastard. Please send checks anyway, because I'm hiring a hit man and taking off for the Bahamas." Then find a bunch of women who have gone through the same thing, compare notes, and head for the tropics, margarita mix in hand.

Beware of the lines guys use to make you feel as if you are wrong for wanting a commitment. They include things like:

- We're too young. No one gets serious with someone these days until they are in their mid-thirties.
- Why did you bring this up? You're giving me "the ultimatum."
- Can't we live together first so we can figure out if this will really work or not?
- I'm just not ready to talk about something like that. I will want to marry you someday, but the time isn't right.
- I can't afford a ring. Why do you put this pressure on me?

The time and location of a breakup can make the split even more of a nightmare than it should be. But remember that if you pay attention to the end-of-the-line signs, you will be able to figure out when things are about to go awry and avoid ending up in many of these precarious situations. However, if by chance you do find yourself breaking up with him through a snorkeling mask in the Pacific, make the most of it and rub him down with chum.

**Sassy Scoop**

If you hear any of these lines, give the guy a wake-up kick. It's your life. You deserve to know where your relationship is going so you can figure out whether you want to stick with him or bury him under the floorboards at Vera Wang.

## The Year at a Glance

There is no good month to go through a breakup, but you can make the most of any season of the year with a little sassy planning.

### January/February

Particularly bad for a breakup because of Valentine's Day, snowy weather, and the post-holiday seasonal blues. However, snow and ice leave wonderful opportunities for revenge. Spray his front steps with water. Freeze his car doors shut and spell out your feelings toward him in the snow in his yard.

### March/April

Spring brings lots of happy couples hanging around outside, and animals mating everywhere. But you can make the most of this season of love by jamming his car windows open before the big spring downpour.

## *May/June*

There are weddings everywhere in the months of May and June, with lots of girls obsessing over invitation fonts and color schemes. However, you can still have fun in this presummer period by tossing a few weed seeds around his front lawn. The summer sun will help them grow tall and strong.

## *July/August*

Hot weather means couples lying on the beach together, reminding you that you're going solo. But the warm weather also means he'll be outside more and thus, will be an easier target for you. If you can't aim and fire with exactitude, accidentally clip the little air conditioner wire that keeps his place icy cool.

## *September/October*

A fall sweater can put any diva in a cozy mood, but only if it is a sweater built for two. Never fear. Halloween is here. You can carry out your revenge schemes in full costume and no one will even raise an eyebrow. Blame the damage on local hooligans. Then pour yourself some spiked cider, and relish your success.

## *November/December*

Thanksgiving, Christmas, and New Year's place unnecessary dating pressure on every single diva's shoulders, but not yours if you use the time to reconnect with your ex's family under the guise of holiday cheer. They'll dish up the latest scoop on your ex's recent screwups, and you'll feel festive in no time.

## Dealing Like a Diva

Unless you've been plotting to get rid of him since the day you met, you will feel sad, surprised, and a bit lost after the breakup. Once you realize what's going on, you won't be sure if it's your heart that's injured, your ego, or both. Remind yourself that what you are feeling at this moment is perfectly okay. There is no "appropriate" reaction or "sane, mature" way to deal with a breakup. There is, however, the diva way.

### Save Face

If you barely reacted when he broke the news, saving face will be easy. You'll just keep your emotions in check whenever he's nearby and he'll continue to think you're doing fine. If by chance you did cry, beg, and plead, however, all is not lost. You can still save face if you let your sassy side inspire you to pull a little attitude when you see him again.

Here are some things you can do that will be more fun than another conversation with him:

- Offer to help set rodent traps in the park.
- Spend a day with a local sanitation worker.
- Attend wakes around town and give your regards.
- Rearrange your nail polish collection by shade.

*A positive attitude may not solve all your problems, but it will annoy enough people to make it worth the effort.*

*—Herm Albright*

- Get a dental cleaning and a good root canal.
- Wait in line to renew your passport and driver's license.
- Try on evening gowns in a store with no air conditioning.
- Translate *War and Peace* into Chinese.
- Collect tossed-out tin cans and cash them in for the nickels.

## *Chase Away Self-Defeating Assumptions*

As soon as he breaks the news, a dreadful little voice will creep out of nowhere and fill your head with silly, unfounded thoughts: "His interest in me was all an act. I am a fat, hairy monster. This breakup is a sign that I am destined to be alone forever." Let your diva side go to work countering these self-defeating assumptions. Replace them with positive ones like "I feel great. He's probably slurping down yet another beer right now with his brainless buddies. I am a goddess on my way to stardom. He will end up a DMV worker." Nip negative thoughts in the bud, because they are not even close to reality.

**Negative thought:** "He's out with another girl right now and they are riding on a steed, her hair flowing in the wind."
**Reality:** He's sitting in a bar watching sports and yelling at the television.

**Negative thought:** "I wasn't good enough for him. He is so wonderful."
**Reality:** He is the devil, occupying your mind. You were too good for him. His mother pays girls to date him and they still won't sleep with him.

**Negative thought:** "He must have been lying when he told me he cares about me."
**Reality:** He does care about you, probably too much to stick

around and let you watch him ignore his brain and follow his . . . how shall we say it . . . below-the-belt brain.

**Negative thought:** "He never really liked me at all. It was all an elaborate lie to get me to sleep with him."
**Reality:** He obviously admired you in some way or he wouldn't have spent time with you. Besides, an "elaborate lie" is not within his range of ability. He had trouble enough proving he didn't eat all the ice cream in the fridge.

**Negative thought:** He got me a crappy gift for my birthday because he didn't like me.
**Reality:** He has really bad taste in presents.

## *Pull Him off the Pedestal*

Dangle him for a while, then drop him to the ground on his ass. Work hard to eliminate from your brain all the admiration and respect you once had for him, if you haven't already. To bring him down fast:

* Grab a couple of extra-thick college-rule notebooks and list every reason why you are better than he is.
* Talk to friends who've always thought he's unattractive, and let them tell you how you've been in a coma.

---

**The Power of Flowers**
To make yourself feel better, by a beautiful bouquet of flowers, let them die quickly, and then send them to him via FedEx with a note marked "Urgent, your fate enclosed."

✳ Separate those things he's promised he will do from the ones he actually followed through on. Note that how much he blabs is inversely proportional to the amount he really accomplishes.

✳ Think of the way he treats others. Recognize that he has the capacity to treat you the same way.

### Don't Do Anything You'll Regret

At the very least, be aware of the consequences you might face if you do something really outrageous, like slice his wee off. (Be careful not to get mixed up and take off his finger by accident). In an emotional flurry, a diva can be spurred to action to chase her ex down with a kitchen knife, make a public scene that hits the news, or get a tattoo that says "behead the bastard." These types of actions, though quite cathartic, can have a lasting impact on your life. Before you decide to make a big huge breakup bang, consider the sequence of events that follow major actions:

✳ Land in jail → post bail money better spent on a fabulous spa day → have criminal record → must endure being asked on dates by local policemen.

✳ Injure ex permanently → ex retaliates → must hire bodyguards for protection → bodyguards scare off good rebound candidates.

✳ Threaten ex with scary phone calls → ex changes phone number making mere aggravating calls impossible → become suspect when ex mysteriously disappears.

✳ Chew out ex loudly in public setting → make front page of paper → must deal with crowds of female fans shouting "go diva go."

*Never attribute to malice what can be adequately explained by stupidity.*

—Nick Diamos

* Destroy ex's house or car → ex gets restraining order → can't get close enough to ex to hit target every time.
* Write ex long letter → ex sells to tabloid → ex makes money off diva.

You don't need the problems that come with an incendiary post-breakup bang. Push his buttons as much as your heart desires, but steer away from anything that you might regret in the long run. He's simply not worth the trouble. You have better things to do, like being fabulous.

### Identify the Ingredients of Your Emotional Cocktail

You might be upset merely because you were in love with him, but sometimes other emotions make the breakup difficult too. If they all mix together, they form one strong emotional cocktail. Identify the ingredients of your post-breakup blues so you can deal with them effectively. They might include any one or more of the following:

* **You caught the "comfort virus."** Sometimes it's hard to break up with someone because you feel so used to the relationship. It's part of your daily routine. But often when you look closer, you realize that life with him is actually no more comfortable than wearing freshly washed jeans. If you're the type of person who thinks a new lunchtime deli feels like an alien planet, you might be more upset about losing the comfort than the guy.

❋ **Your ego is bruised.** You weren't even sure you liked him to begin with, but you still can't believe he doesn't worship you. You feel dumb and embarrassed. If you really don't care about him but the breakup is still making you insane, you are suffering from a big old ego bruise. In that case you're in luck, because ego bruises heal much faster than a broken heart.

❋ **You hate being single.** You'd rather be in a bad relationship than go solo again. You hate finding dates to events, making plans for the weekend, and fielding annoying questions from family members who are trying to pair you off. You couldn't care less whether you're dating him or Tattoo from *Fantasy Island*. You just want a warm body to play the part of boyfriend.

Any number of emotions can compound your feelings of angst during a breakup. Once you identify them, it will be easier to get over him. You will learn how to deal with emotions and more in the chapters that follow, but for now work on recognizing the ingredients in your own personal emotional cocktail.

### Think Before Agreeing to Be "Friends"

The "let's be friends" agreement is a pact made by both parties in 75 percent of all breakups (*Worthless Pact Manual*). What does it mean? Think about it: Your friends loan you disco music, accompany you to chick flicks, and share your fetish for

*Never hit a man with glasses. Hit him with something bigger and heavier.*

—*Anonymous*

bargain-basement shopping. Is he going to become like them? If so, get to work on finding him an undereye concealer that will hide those heinous dark circles he's sporting, and a good pedicure to save his nasty feet. You've got to do *something* to make him a presentable wing woman.

These things are probably not what your ex has in mind when he suggests friendship. In fact, he probably doesn't even know what he has in mind. Post-breakup "friendship" usually amounts to a few awkward lunches and the guy telling the girl things about his life that make her cringe—not an association worthy of your time.

As the queen of sass, you do not have to settle for this typical version of friendship. You can tell him you'll be friends with him but never follow up, or you can arrange a short-term friendship in which he agrees to give you easy access to his house, car, and

---

**Friend-to-Friend Tips**

Share this helpful, friendly housekeeping advice with your ex.

- If he adds one cup of bleach to his laundry, he can wash the whites and darks together without ruining his clothes.
- Nail polish remover will take the bird droppings off the hood of his shiny red car.
- He no longer needs to use household cleansers in a well-ventilated area because the fumes, in moderate doses, are actually good for his hair loss.
- The metal containers you gave him for his birthday are microwave safe.
- His computer keyboard will work better if he washes it in the tub.

*Man is the only animal that can remain on friendly terms with the victims he intends to eat until he eats them.*

—*Samuel Butler*

personal belongings. Then, in addition to the awkward lunches, you can at least use his stuff, find great blackmail material, and give him helpful advice in the areas where he needs it most.

Being fabulous is a full-time job. If he's not part of the process he's in the way, so only agree to friendship after thinking it through and making sure it will add something to your busy life.

### Crawl Inside His Head

Take a few minutes to do this hokey little exercise. It will help relieve some of the shock of the breakup by giving you insight into his mind.

✳ Find a quiet location. If necessary, layer the room with acoustic soundproofing material to drown out the yapping of your roommates.

✳ Sit back, relax, and think of all the reasons why *you* might break up with a guy. He's cute but you don't feel passionate enough about him; he's just a fun friend and you want more out of a relationship; he's smart and energetic, but you don't think he would jell with you in the long term; he is kind and loving, but a lazy ass.

✳ Next, project this thinking onto your guy and you will be able to step inside his head for just a minute. It's empty in there, right? Isn't it great! You can fit your entire body inside without a problem and look around for clues.

Once you're inside, you'll probably see that he has needs that can't be met if he stays in the relationship. It's not up to you to solve his problems or define his needs, but it may help you take the finale less personally and keep your composure if you can understand his motivation. Remember, he may not even be aware of some of these motives for wanting to split.

### Career

He wants his career in order before he settles down. Though women are clever and can deal with more than one demand on our time, men suffer from tunnel vision. They have problems juggling many responsibilities at once. If he's into building his career, his brain can explode if a serious girlfriend is added to the mix.

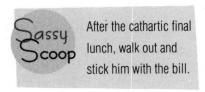

Sassy Scoop

After the cathartic final lunch, walk out and stick him with the bill.

### Women

He doesn't have it in him to stay with one girl. The classic playboy moves from woman to woman. Even when he's disgusting and old, he still thinks he's a stud. He combs that one strand of hair over his bald spot and drives his Jaguar into town, winking at the beauties.

### Doing His Own Thing

He has specific long-term interests or needs different from your own. Maybe he wants to move to Europe for ten years and he knows you don't. Maybe he wants raunchy sex every day for the rest of his life and thinks he would be better off marrying a prostitute. He might know he doesn't feel strongly enough about the relationship to give you the love and dedication you deserve. Remember—you'll never change him. You can't dye white pants blue and expect them to turn out looking like really cool jeans. Just find the jeans and buy two pairs. It never hurts to have a backup.

### Time

Some guys feel like they need a certain amount of time being young and living it up on the singles scene. They don't want to get serious with a girl until they reach the age they think is "right." If his friends are all single and he's still spending most of his nights out at bars, it is likely he is not mature enough yet to commit seriously to a woman.

### Insanity

Some guys are just plain messed up, and their very nature precludes them from staying involved with a woman. If he is a little off his rocker, unreliable, into drugs and alcohol or self-destructive in any way, he can't have a successful relationship with a woman. In fact, he probably can't even hold a steady job or take care of his basic needs on a regular basis. Do not take on the responsibility of trying to change him or play shrink. Chances are he will not change without some cataclysmic event prompting a major life transformation. A mere kick in the ass won't suffice.

## Navigating Extreme Schmuckdom

With most men, there is a logical reason why they are initiating a breakup, one that does not warrant punishment beyond

*He is one of those people who would be enormously improved by death.*

*—H. H. Munro (Saki)*

> *Before you criticize someone, you should walk a mile in their shoes. That way, when you criticize them, you are a mile away from them, and you have their shoes.*
>
> —Frieda Norris

the basic sassy maneuvers. For other men, the only reason is extreme schmuckdom. Extreme schmuckdom is a state in which a guy does something so awful that he deserves pain, torture, and lifelong anguish (instead of merely pain and torture).

If you are a diva dealing with this type of guy, you might feel even more incensed than others, but you are actually in a most fortunate position. You have narrowly escaped spending your life with one of the world's biggest losers. That calls for a little champagne.

Many women are not so lucky. Once you start thinking about the scumbag's behavior, you'll actually be thrilled to see him go. If you are not sure if your ex qualifies as a big schmuck, a few telltale situations are listed here to help you decide:

### He Cheated

If he cheated on you, he is a bona fide schmuck. Realize that he will probably cheat on women for years to come. At least you got rid of him early. Pin a blinking sign on his head and save the rest of womankind from his evil ways. If you're not sure if he's cheating, find out by equipping his briefcase with a microscopic recorder. Or you could simply ask him, and then watch the slug squirm and avoid eye contact. There is no excuse for cheating under any circumstances. A guy who does so lacks integrity and, therefore, has no right to be breathing.

### He Lied

We're not talking little white lies, e.g., he got the necklace he gave you free because his friend's cousin is a jeweler. We're talking big, fat, ugly lies. Though no lie is good, obviously, some will earn him the schmuck title and others are simply human. Learn the difference by studying the following examples.

**Little white lie:** Using "I had a doctor's appointment" to cover his search for your birthday gift.

**Schmuck lie:** Using "I had a doctor's appointment" to cover his date with a doctor.

**Little white lie:** Saying "She's just an old friend" when you run into a girl that he used to date.

**Schmuck lie:** Saying "She's just an old friend" when he's been e-mailing her every day for six months.

**Little white lie:** Claiming "I have to work Saturday" when your annoying roommate from college is in town.

**Schmuck lie:** Claiming "I have to work Saturday" when your parents are in town and your mother can't wait to meet him.

**Little white lie:** Insisting "I'm the same age you are," when he's a year younger.

**Schmuck lie:** Insisting "I'm the same age you are," when he's got five years or more on either side.

**Little white lie:** Saying, "I've never used drugs before in my life," when he's tried marijuana once or twice.

**Schmuck lie:** Saying, "I've never used drugs before in my life," when he has a mysterious white powder crusted on his nose.

### He Is a Criminal

If he's peddling drugs, robbing banks, or abducting kids, he is beyond schmuck. Also included in this category is any kind of abuse, physical or verbal. Remember that name-calling, yelling, manipulation, and other verbal behaviors also qualify as abuse when your ex does them to you. A guy who does these things should not be allowed to see the light of the free world again. Of course, if you do them to him, it's just good solid diva fun.

The first step in breakup recovery is to face the end with courage and remind yourself that you can keep going no matter how difficult things seem. You've dealt with the finale, reviewed potential explanations for the breakup, and thought about how serious of a punishment he deserves. Now it's time to move on and cope with the challenges of the weeks that follow. The next chapter will help you get through the aftermath with sass and then arise victorious, fine jewelry and a few of his belongings in hand.

> There will come a time when you believe everything is finished.
> That will be the beginning.
> —Louis L'Amour . . .
> of his hell on earth (Sassy Diva).

# Chapter Two

# Lose the Guy, Keep the Jewelry

The days that follow the breakup are critical. This period is an extension of the finale. It's when you wrap things up, return personal belongings to each other, and make final decisions regarding anything else you shared. Continue to deal like a diva and make these moments work for you. Though you inevitably feel very emotional, this is a great opportunity to clear your head and leave the relationship with more than just his dirty laundry and a few pictures.

## Clean House

When a diva leaves a relationship, she cleans house. She seizes the moment, wipes away the dirt and garbage her ex left behind, and moves on. This section will help you get rid of his things and reclaim yours with style—while providing a much-needed etiquette lesson on division of property after the big split.

*Cleaning Essentials*

Before you drive the U-Haul over to his place to drop of his garbage and take away those things you rightfully deserve, gather the cleaning supplies you'll need to do the deed.

✳ **Rubber gloves:** Wear them to sift through the crap in his sty. Never risk contracting a disease from the festering piles of crud lying around his place.

✳ **Liquid bleach:** While there, fill the nozzle of his steam iron.

✳ **Hardwood polish or oil:** He likes his work pants clean, so use this to wipe them down 'til they're golden brown.

✳ **Steel-wool scrubber:** An unparalleled exfoliator for tough male skin. Leave it in his bathroom next to his soap.

✳ **Toilet brush:** His toothbrush will do just fine. Swish it around in the toilet so it's extra fresh when he uses it that night.

✳ **Bucket:** Collect the little things you love best, like his universal remote control and "Girls Gone Wild" video collection. Tuck them away in your handy bucket.

✳ **Folding stepladder:** For reaching those items up high, like his prized beer-bottle collection. Oh, my gosh—so clumsy of you!

✳ **Shovel:** Keep a shovel nearby to clean up after he spews out lines of bullshit. While you have it out, give him a little crack over the head too. Sticks and stones may break his bones, but a shovel will knock him unconscious.

✳ **Pencil and paper:** A pencil and paper are essential in any cleaning kit. Jot down the gas mileage from your trip and submit it to him for reimbursement. While you're at it, give him receipts for any dresses you bought with him in mind.

## *Reclaim Your Starlet Stash*

Once you have your cleaning supplies in order, you are ready to reclaim those things that are your own and give him back his bag of trash. Getting back your belongings should be the easiest part of breaking up. Traditional breakup gurus will tell you to make sure you get back every last thing so you have no reason to see him again. This slice of advice is up for debate. If you have the opportunity, you can always leave the CD you played during intimate moments in an obscure location in his apartment. This planted item will come in handy down the road. Three months later, when you look and feel great, you can swing by to pick it up—with your new boyfriend at your side, of course.

## *Kindly Return His Garbage*

Don't spend too much time gathering his things to give back to him. If his place is typically messy, he doesn't notice what's missing anyway. It's not your job to search high and low for his junk-drawer goodies. However, returning his junk can be an excellent opportunity to clear your own place of unwanted clutter. Slide his boxers and T-shirt right in with your old toaster and the lone paper clips, pennies, and Chinese fortunes sitting in your kitchen drawer. Of course, find the right fortune to bury in his boxers, such as "You are a small man with a dismal future." Cover the box and shove it his way.

> Always pay debts to your ex in full in shiny pennies. Borrow a large truck, load up that $1,000 you owe him, and dump it on his lawn.
>
> **Sassy Scoop**

### Previously Exchanged Gifts

When it comes to previously exchanged gifts, you have to make a strategic decision. Did you give him better presents than he gave you? If so, ask for everything back. If, however, he gave you diamond earrings and a cashmere sweater, but you only bought him a Homer Simpson tie, let him keep his gifts. He'll take your lead and let you keep yours too. If he does ask you to return a prized item, any of the following excuses will work just fine.

* How awful! I loaned that sweater to my friend from work and unfortunately, the company transferred her to a small, remote village in Siberia before she could return it.

* Is that the thing my mom used to clean the bathroom when she came to visit? Oh my gosh. I'm so sorry.

* Oh, that little thing? I didn't realize it was real. I donated it to a wilderness charity when I was on a trip in Appalachia.

* You never gave that to me, did you? I remember receiving a sort of ugly, ratty shirt from you, but not the nice one you're describing.

* I'm so absent-minded. I just can't remember where I put your stuff. Let me check the garbage and get back with you.

If you know he's the type to feel guilty, try the "Oh, I really shouldn't keep it" routine. "Oh, I really shouldn't

> Whereas women of old had to sell their ex's gifts and belongings at garage sales, technology has blessed the modern diva with online auction sites. Try shipping an ex's favorite football jersey to a complete stranger for less than $5. It is pure satisfaction.
>
> Sassy Scoop

keep this precious stone necklace. It is my favorite, but you did pay for it." Reverse psychology works nicely with a remorseful man, but before going with this option, make sure he's gullible enough to fall for it. Otherwise, you might end up giving things back that could yield a healthy sum at the local pawnshop.

### Shared Items and Freebies

While you have him in giving mode, vie for a few freebies—those items of his that you love to use. His cozy flannel pajama bottoms, his Discman, and his 32-inch flat-screen TV can all be yours with the help of a strong friend and large moving van. Why spend a dime when Ex-Boyfriends-R-Us is open twenty-four hours a day, and everything is free?

The golden rule of breaking up is that the jackass in the relationship must concede all shared items to the blameless partner. The only exception to this rule is a shared living creature. Is the fluffy poodle more his or yours? One of you probably has primary ownership and obviously, that person should get to keep the animal. If you can't decide, split it. Give him the upper half because he needs the brain more. You keep the ass so you don't miss him.

When faced with a dispute over shared items, let him have anything that is easy to replace. The more time you spend arguing, the less time you have left in your life to ruin his. One

*I am a marvelous housekeeper. Every time I leave a man, I keep his house.*

—Zsa Zsa Gabor

**Always Leave Your Mark**
Be sure to hug him goodbye after dropping off his stuff.
Nuzzle in close and wipe a little oil-based foundation or
red all-day lipstick on his shirt.

other quick and easy solution is to destroy "by accident" anything
in question. Leaving it under the wheel of a parked tractor-trailer
works every time.

## Blame Him, Defame Him

You've talked it out, retrieved your things, and said your goodbyes. Now it's time for the final step in recovery, stage one. Use
your remaining energy to rally friends, family, and everyone in his
life to your side. The first twenty-four hours of a breakup are so
overwhelming that the only thing you will probably be able to do
is recount the story to friends, your mother, your aunt, and even
the lady who cuts your hair. But you've got to move fast. If you
can throw his siblings, his mother, and his close friends into this
mix, you will have an entire army behind you before he even
wakes up the next morning. With your emotions running high
and his shortcomings on the tip of your tongue, it won't be hard
to gain their sympathies. These people are your ruin-his-life
cheerleaders. They will make you feel loved and come to your aid
when you want him to find out about your multimillion-dollar
lottery win or your engagement to his old boss.

In order to draw a crowd into your ring, you'll need a command center. This center should contain, at the very least, a
phone, a box of tissues, and e-mail access. If you have these items

at home, it's not a bad place to set up operations. An even better location is the pad of a good, straight male friend who you suspect has a secret crush on you. Turn him into post-breakup man-slave and he'll offer you free drinks, food, and the technology you need to get the word out to everyone. Meanwhile, he'll lavish you with praise, remind you that you're skinny and beautiful, and tell you how much he hated your ex. This attention is exactly what you need to regain your composure and get to work building the troops.

Crowd rallying is an important component of breakup recovery. If done correctly, each person will offer unique criticisms of your ex and make you feel lucky he's gone. They will also rise to red alert, keeping one foot on the gas at all times just in case he walks by. Remember—you will need these supportive

### The Family Frenzy

Do you have an annoying sibling who will tease you instead of coming to your aid? If so, try one of the following snappy remarks to put the less-favored child in his or her place:

- Shut the hell up, wench/ass. At least I am not dating a blowup doll, like someone else in our family.
- Jealous because you look like Uncle Bert and you're hairy like him, too?
- Do you know Mom and Dad's will specifies a slightly lower percentage for you? That's because they don't like you.
- Mom always talks about how she should have stopped after me. (If you're older.)
- Dad says I'm proof that they certainly do save the best for last. (If you're younger.)

friends in the future to tout your successes when your ex is around. Win them over now. Then, in a few weeks, when you ask them to paint graffiti on his car, they will be ready and willing, fluorescent paint cans in hand.

## *His Family and Friends*

Even if you despise his parents and think his sister is an ugly wench, call them to say goodbye. Don't do it because it's proper; to hell with that. Call them because they are assets you can use in the future. Secure their sympathies now before he gets to them with his side of the story. If you are on neutral or outstanding terms with his family, you are in luck. You have a network of spies to give you information about his life and torment him on your behalf. Get to work on winning them over immediately. Muster every tear and kind word you can, and pour on the charm. If you play your cards right, his mother will badger him incessantly and ask him questions about the breakup. She'll make sure he knows he's making a mistake. Then his sister will chime in with how much she's going to miss you. She'll probably add that you are too good for him anyway and that he's an idiot who will never meet another girl. And that's just the beginning!

**Photo Op**
Place yourself in the center of all his family photographs at important events like weddings and anniversary parties, and be sure to show a little leg. After the breakup, his family will always remember you when they see your shining smile in the colorful 8" × 10" glossies.

Benefits of Befriending His Family

* His mother will ask him about you every day and compare his new girlfriends to you.

* His father will slip up and call his new girlfriends by your name.

* You will be able to give his siblings regular updates on your wonderful life and they will pass the word along to him with a nostalgic sigh.

* You will be able to send big, splashy holiday cards to his family every year just so he has to look at them on the mantel when he goes home for the holidays.

* His family will keep you informed of his failures. Once they convey dozens of acts of stupidity, you will see him for the loser he is.

* If he ever gets married, his family will badger him to invite you to his wedding. His mother might even add, "Too bad you didn't stick with someone nice like her."

If his family never liked you, your lip service probably won't do much good. Look at the bright side; at least you never have to see them again—

By this time you've taken the first steps toward full recovery, but you still have some hard times ahead. It definitely takes a few weeks or more to get through the initial shock and grieving that accompany a breakup. Just remember that you will do it. No phase in life lasts forever. For right now, relax and be sad for a while, but try to remember that the sassy side of you is there even if it is in hibernation. You are fabulous, confident, and able to handle this breakup. Things might not always seem that way, but with each day that passes, you will feel a little bit better.

Sassy Scoop

*If you are going through hell,
keep going.*

—Sir Winston Churchill

unless you marry his brother, a wonderful revenge technique, though one with obvious consequences. A healthier alternative to bonding yourself in marriage to his brother, however, is to move on. Eventually you'll find someone who is not related to him who will love and respect you. But don't forget your experience with your ex. Learn from your mistakes, capitalize on your failures, and move on with style.

## The Lingering Ex

As you learned in Chapter 1, you must commit to the idea that the relationship is over for good before you can begin the recovery process. Perhaps you've already done so and there is no question in your mind that he is last year's crop. Nevertheless, the lingering ex sometimes finds his way back again and leaves you wondering just how "over" the relationship really is. Don't let these ambiguous moves put you back at square one. Recognize them so you can put a stop to them promptly and continue on the road to stardom.

**A Friendly Smile**—You see him in a bar and he looks at you just like he used to when you were dating.

**The Random Stop-Over**—You're adorned in towels and wearing a plastic hairnet from a highlighting kit. Your doorbell rings and there he is. He just stopped by to say "hello."

**The Drunken Midnight Ring**—You dream that your alarm clock is going off, but you wake up to find that your phone is ringing. You answer it thinking a friend is having a crisis. Instead, you hear his slobbering voice on the other end.

**Confusing Comments to Friends**—You get an e-mail from your best buddy. "I ran into him and he told me he really misses you."

**The Birthday Card Signed "Love"**—Your own parents send a card late, but his shows up on the very day signed with a lopsided heart etched in pen.

Don't go crazy trying to figure out what it all means—you've got better things to do with your time than trying to decipher the inner workings of his guppy brain. Truth be told, he might not even be aware of the fact that his behavior is ambiguous. He might think he's "being nice." Even if he is aware, all the analysis in the world won't give you an answer to the question "Why?" In fact, taping his phone calls and playing them backward will likely yield nothing more than "I worship Satan." (Isn't that how the urban legend goes?) So don't waste time trying to figure him out. He's already proved that he is nothing more than a weed in your flowery life. You will feel much better when you pull him out by the roots, stomp on him, and then throw him in the garbage. Put a stop to his confusing behavior for good with some of these tactics:

* Have a male friend record the outgoing message on your answering machine.

* Purchase personalized mugs, one that has your name and one that says "Dick." Serve him coffee in the "Dick" mug when he pops by for a visit.

* Form a phallic centerpiece by planting two ball-shaped cactuses alongside a tall one. If he shows up at your place, tell him he caught you just about to "trim the cactus." Take a huge knife and slice off the tip forcefully. It is not standard practice to trim a cactus, but he'll never know.

✱ Toss a rubber roach in with the birthday card and mark the envelope "return to sender."

✱ Point out the large, green leafy substance between his teeth when he smiles at you.

✱ Have your friends counter his comments with "Last time I talked to her, she didn't even mention your name."

Recovering from a breakup is hard enough without him interrupting the grieving process with his confusing behavior. Remember the "Sassy Rules" from Chapter 1. If there's any chance of getting back together, he has to tell you explicitly that he's interested in starting over with you, and then only after he's apologized for his behavior and proved that he will behave respectfully the next time around. Ambiguous moves are a violation of the sassy rule and a waste of your time. Make it clear that you want him to stop what he's doing, and then close the door forever. Just be sure his finger is caught in it when you do.

> **Before it's finally over, he has a right to know if:**
>
> • You were faking it during intimate moments.
> • Your father thought he was your outreach case.
> • His brother hit on you last Thanksgiving.
> • Working out never did him any good.
> • You really hated the necklace he bought you.
> • You hated his mother, sister, dog, or all three.
> • Your friends thought you could do better.

## Peculiar Predicaments

As if a lingering ex isn't difficult enough to deal with, sometimes other factors complicate the recovery process. If you were in a "less traditional" relationship—he was married, or was your boss, your roommate, etc.—you'll have to jump over a few additional hurdles

**Just Don't Do It**

Out of respect for other divas in the universe, never date a married man. Karma dictates that if you do, one day your actions will come back to you. You don't need that kind of hassle in life.

before closing the door on the past. However, these peculiar predicaments don't have to stand in the way of your recovery. Just know the unique challenges they entail, and handle them like a diva.

### The Married Guy

Dating a married man is not exactly easy, nor is breaking up with one. This isn't only because he has a family; more important, he is at heart a cheater. A man who cheats on his wife will also cheat on his girlfriend, and probably cheats in dozens of other circumstances in his life. If you'd hung in there long enough, most likely one day you would have been on the receiving end of the cheating. A cheater is a bona fide schmuck, so thank your lucky stars that he went back home, and wish for the best for the poor woman who has to deal with him forever.

### The Workplace Romance

A workplace breakup can become a daily nightmare you can't escape if you don't keep it under control. You start each day with a cup of coffee and a fresh kick in the stomach when you see his face. No diva needs an ex staring at her while she's at her desk plotting her rise to power. If your ex was your boss, the only thing you can do is leave right away. No matter how much the two of you talk it through, your career and your recovery are at stake if you keep working for him. Don't forget to tell HR in your exit interview about him pilfering tape and reams of paper.

If your ex is a coworker or underling, you have a little more leeway to stay and see if you can deal with him being around all day long. But a major key to recovery is getting him out of your head. That's kind of difficult when you have to see him every ten minutes. So ultimately, if you can leave, you should. If you have any say in choosing your replacement, select an equally sassy woman so you can be sure she'll fix him good.

### A *Family Affair*

Dating a friend's brother—and then having him break up with you—comes with its own unique challenges. Because those around you already know him, you will have to put extra effort into rallying people to your side. If he's truly a big jackass, even his sister should see his true colors. You could try to convince her to sleep around with his friends to get back at him, but corrupting a fellow goddess in the name of revenge is not the diva way. Just ruin him directly.

### *Fresh Young Thing*

The younger guy is easy to break up with because there is a logical explanation for his actions that does not implicate the diva: he's immature. Dating a younger guy is like having a teenage son. When you want to go to dinner, he wants to grab a hotdog at the hotdog factory. When you are aching to spend a Friday night watching a Broadway play, he is doing a keg stand at the frat house down the street. A younger guy is so immature that you cannot possibly take anything he does seriously or personally. To

*I never hated a man enough to give him his diamonds back.*

—Zsa Zsa Gabor

fix his ass, erase his high score on his video games or leave his beer in the sun. Teaching him a lesson should be quite simple. You have several to choose from, given he has so many left to learn.

## Living Together

If you live with your ex, you probably have a very severe case of the comfort virus. Put on a shoe with a pointed, sharp toe and kick him out onto the curb immediately. If you can't do that because of some little obstacle—like if he owns the place—move today. Money, time, and trouble are no object in a post-breakup move. If you really can't do it right now, at least construct a concrete wall and shackle him behind it until you can.

If you are living with him, make a list of the specific challenges you will face, along with the actions you plan to take to tackle them head-on. Your list might look something like this:

**Problem:** You have all of the same friends, and now they have to take sides.
**Solution:** Get to them before he does so their choice is obvious.

**Problem:** You're not used to dealing with all expenses on your own.
**Solution:** Make him foot the bill for a few months. After all, he's the jackass who initiated the breakup.

**Problem:** You don't have the time and energy to shop around for an affordable place.
**Solution:** Take the first place you find that's nice, and have him write the check.

**Problem:** It takes a while to receive separate mail and phone calls and to ensure that other critical information is sent to each of you.
**Solution:** Be happy knowing that telemarketers will call him asking for you for years to come, and junk mail with your name on it will fill his mailbox.

No matter what your peculiar predicament is, you can handle this breakup with style because you are a fabulous diva. First get back what's yours. Then make sure you don't let him ride off into the sunset without paying handsomely for the pain and suffering he's caused. Let your sassy side dictate your moves in every situation, and you'll walk away with a wealth of experience, a feeling of triumph, and a few free goodies to boot.

# Chapter Three
# Grieve-a Like a Diva

The time immediately following a breakup is long and grueling. Minutes seem like days; days seem like decades. You can't eat or sleep. You finish off an entire family-size box of tissues in record time and then resort to the few crumpled ones you find in a coat pocket. Your friends and family rally around to help you through your rough time. They call to check in and help analyze your hellish ordeal. They even tell you to call in the middle of the night if you need to.

Then one day nobody calls. When you dial a number, it goes straight to voice mail. Your best friend is on a business trip in Switzerland. Your mom is planting new shrubs outside and can't hear the phone. You run to your computer every time it makes the "new mail" sound to find nothing more than another piece of Viagra spam. Nobody is left to help you, but you still aren't better. Your breakup entourage has moved on to the next crisis, leaving you alone on the red carpet in your favorite flannel pajamas. Now that you have this time to yourself, away from the drama and fanfare of the post-breakup limelight, it's time to reconnect with yourself and move on to the next phase in breakup survival. So, put on your favorite CD, break out your diary, and take a little more time to bawl your eyes out—alone.

## Motivational Crying

You've probably noticed already that unless you are Superwoman, you are not going to get through the breakup experience without a fair share of crying. Embrace it. It's an integral part of the healing process, and though it's not pleasant, it is cleansing.

Some women may choose to act out their despair and frustration in public, but many of us do the majority of post-breakup crying at home, where we can plead with his picture, reread old e-mails, and plot his demise in private, laying the relationship to rest in our own special way. Breakup experts call this process crying-inspired progress. However, sassy divas everywhere prefer the term "motivational crying." It is a form of emotional release that will get you back on your feet quickly so you can trample him with ease the next time you see him.

If you are crying more now than you did at first, do not fear. You aren't getting worse. You are experiencing a very annoying, yet very normal, emotional healing process. Breaking up is a lot like going for a 10-mile run after lying in a lawn chair on the beach for six months. Your muscles are numb the first day or two, but after a week you can't walk, step into the shower, or sit on the toilet without excruciating pain.

*Crying is fun . . . when he's the one doing it.*

*—Anonymous*

As the shock fades and the sore breakup muscles kick in, you may find comfort in the trite little phrase, "That which doesn't kill us makes us stronger." Or perhaps the slightly less well known variation, "He who doesn't strengthen us makes us kill." While you probably don't want to actually end your ex's life and deal with the inconvenient legal consequences, you can still use this experience to build your strength and regain the upper hand.

Grief is motivational for a diva because she tackles it by taking action and moving forward in her life. You will never be immune from life's problems and challenges (nor will your ex, a comforting thought), but you can learn to deal with them successfully and arise stronger for the wear. This post-breakup period is not easy, but if you continue to take action and face each day with enthusiasm, before long you will look at his picture and ask, "Why in the world did I date him?"

> Time and again, magazines recommend hemorrhoid cream as a way to make your teary, swollen eyes look fresh and happy again. There's something kind of scary about wiping that crap on your face. So instead, buy it in bulk and dip your ex in it headfirst. Watch the big hemorrhoid vanish, and your tears right along with him.
>
> Sassy Scoop

If you find yourself crying in public, at places like work or school, try one of these handy excuses to divert annoying questions:

- I used my felt-tip pen as eyeliner by accident.
- I splashed my face with water so I don't doze during your morning presentation/lecture.
- This new "moist and creamy" eye shadow is a lot more moist than I bargained for.
- Or the tried and true: My entire family died in a gruesome accident this morning. Thanks for asking.

## Adopt a "Take Action" Attitude

Traditional breakup philosophy states that the best way to get through the grieving process is to "soothe your soul" (whatever that means). This phrase conjures images of slow music, dim lights, and aromatic candles. On the contrary, a sassy chick doesn't listen to slow, sappy music after a breakup. She puts "Maneater" on repeat and makes up a revenge dance. She doesn't burn aromatic candles unless they're part of a spell or a way to get his smelly-ass scent out of the room.

Nothing is worse after a breakup than endless quiet time and solitude. To get through this difficult period, you need to spend more time "doing" than worrying. This is the core of a "take action" attitude. It's fine if you want to stay in bed for a little while and stare at the ceiling. But after you've taken a few days to mourn his loss, it is time to stockpile artillery and do the other things you need to do to regain your energy and start coping.

### An Action Plan to Get You over Any Man

To pull yourself out of the doldrums, develop an action plan and then commit to sticking to it even when the going gets tough. Your own personal action plan can be made up of anything you want as long as it involves getting up and getting out the door. If you don't know where to begin, follow these steps. You'll be moving in the right direction in no time.

*Always forgive your enemies— nothing annoys them so much.*

*—Oscar Wilde*

**Getting Perspective**

Pretend a friend of yours is in your shoes. How would you help her get through the breakup? What decisions would you encourage her to make? What things would you see about her relationship that she doesn't? Try to be this objective about your own breakup. A situation always appears clearer to those who are not in it.

1. **Make a list of the most disgustingly happy people you know**—the coworkers who are chipper at 8 A.M., your rosy-cheeked friends who always have a perky perspective, and those sugar-sweet people who bombard you with happy e-mail forwards.

2. **Pick one of the people off the list and, annoying though she may be, take a clue from her.** Her happy perspective and problem-solving philosophies are good to have on hand, should you need them. Watch her closely and see what she does when she's feeling down. Does she make time for herself? Get enough sleep? Reward herself with chocolate fudge ice cream every couple of days? See if you can learn something about her coping strategies that you can use yourself.

3. **Develop a game plan to do something productive each day.** Determine what you can do to spice up your life, solve your problems, and move yourself to a happier place. The bulk of your plan should be things you are going to do for you, but it's okay to throw on a few things for your ex, too, like "buy him super glue lip balm" or "sign him up for a lobotomy." Once you have your game plan together, muster all of your enthusiasm and spring into action.

*Life is not the way it is supposed to be. It is the way it is. The way you cope with it makes the difference.*

*—Virginia Satir*

Do at least one productive thing each day. Focusing on a productive task is an excellent way to take your mind off the breakup.

## Rebound Relief

A great way to get over any guy is to meet a new one. A good rebound man will give you a quick ego boost, a healthy dose of physical contact, and something to focus on for the short term while you're getting over your ex. He'll also be an excellent asset to your revenge plan. Once your ex catches wind of your new relationship he'll be certain you've moved on, and you will no longer be a suspect when his magazines are missing or his lawn is covered with fragrant fertilizer.

A rebound guy will also remind you of how easy it is for you, a fabulous diva, to meet men if you wish. Whereas your ex will have to attack women in a bar while simultaneously dealing with his breakup baggage, you can effortlessly attract great guys simply by grabbing a drink and looking confident. Of course, you'll have to deal with the

Though it is important to "stop and smell the roses" sometimes, not every "now" is worth sniffing. After the breakup, forget about today. Think about tomorrow, and what you're going to do to make it amazing. Confine your rose-smelling to the black ones you're sending anonymously to his office.

Sassy Scoop

rabble too, but somewhere among the slimy bar crowd there's always a perfect rebound candidate. When you are evaluating your options, consider the following essential qualities.

A good rebound guy is:

... good-looking but a little bit of an airhead. Any himbo will do just fine.

... has the cash to take you out to fun places and to restaurants where your ex might see you.

... a player, a musician, a professional athlete, or some other "type" that you might not want a relationship with under any other circumstances. A rebound guy is the perfect opportunity to experiment, to taste a flavor of ice cream with no obligation to buy the entire half-gallon.

... issue-free, or at least doesn't tell you about his problems. Only guys with a sense of humor and a bright outlook on life qualify for the rebound position.

... fun-loving. If he can't spin you to the cheesiest tune, he is not in the running. Your rebound man must be ready to have a ball and bring you along for the ride.

Avoid the rebound guy who is:

... easily hurt. You don't want to rip the poor guy's heart in two by dumping him three weeks after you start dating him.

> *Even if it doesn't work, there is something healthy and invigorating about direct action.*
>
> —Henry Miller

Focus on ripping up your ex's heart, but find a rebound guy who is tough as nails.

. . . an ax murderer. While it's true that you can show much less discretion with a rebound guy—a male model with no brain will fill your needs—don't lower the bar too far or you might end up with a scary guy who is worse than your ex, and dangerous too.

. . . a good friend that you really have absolutely no genuine interest in. Don't bother ruining a good friendship for a post-breakup Band-Aid.

. . . going through a breakup too. Two rebounds do not make a right. You do not need a guy with sob stories or an obsession with his ex. The point of a rebound guy is that he provides a fun, light fling that gets you through the tough times. He can't be a bandage for your wounds if he can't dress his own.

. . . a sex fiend. If you want to sleep with your rebound guy, that's your business. But he should not be pressuring you to do it like an aggressive animal. Though all men are a bit sex-obsessed, avoid a rebound guy that admits to it outright.

While a rebound guy may not end up being the man of your dreams, he will provide relief from the breakup and get your mind rolling in a new direction. So keep your eyes open for him wherever you go. When he appears, have him buy you a drink.

## The Dynamic Diva Duo

If you're not up for a rebound man, or you're just looking for some girl time, to really grieve-a like a diva, you will need at least one competent and experienced accomplice to stick by your side and help you along. The two of you will form an invincible post-breakup dynamic duo. An accomplice is someone you can spill all

**Friends and Enemies**
The enemy of your enemy is your friend and an excellent accomplice.

of your feelings to comfortably. She is there to accept your frequent phone calls, to listen to you sob, and to help you make sense of this situation. When you hate someone, your accomplice hates him too. She wants to see your ex suffer and reminds you of all the annoying things about him that you've forgotten. This girl is the ultimate co-conspirator.

## *The A-List Accomplice*

To carry out the breakup recovery mission successfully, you will need a partner-in-crime with skills that complement your own and make your team invincible. Look for some or all of the following qualities in your all-star accomplice:

✻ **She commits acts as bad as or worse than you do during a breakup.** She will help you find humor in the situation. When you sign him up for mailings from the local gay bar, she'll cheer you on. She'll also be able to offer a few strategies of her own.

✻ **She agrees with you that he's a bastard but will also agree with you if you decide to forgive him.** She has great faith in your ability to judge character and understands the emotional seesaw you're on right now. If you want her to bump him off, she'll get to work on it immediately. If you then change your mind, she won't complain about all the work she's gone through to set up the hit.

✱ **She is shrewd, smart, and technically competent.** She knows enough to switch off the caller ID function when she pranks him. She understands how to operate voice mail so she can figure out when he last checked his messages. She knows that a few fire ants can go a long way if they are placed discreetly in his favorite gym shorts.

✱ **She doesn't care how others perceive her.** She will gladly set off his car alarm during the big basketball game or point out his beer gut. She'll tell him you're dating a hot new guy who runs his own company, won a Congressional election, and can bench-press 300 pounds. Then she'll laugh with you as she describes the look on his face and the disgusting girl he was with, who had extremely visible panty line.

✱ **She has sass, nerve, and an edge.** She speaks up on your behalf and counters blasphemous rumors about the breakup. If you run into him unexpectedly, this friend will deal with him for you while you hide in a bathroom stall. She will also help you run into him intentionally once or twice—maybe with a rugged-terrain vehicle.

An A-List Accomplice Can . . .

✱ Watch to see if he's coming while you slip a shot of Tabasco sauce in his drink.

✱ Drive by his house and throw a few rocks on his lawn.

✱ Call you on your cell phone if you're in his presence so you can cheerfully say, "Gotta run! Late for my dinner date."

✱ Deal with other people so you don't have to give them a play-by-play of the breakup.

✱ Deliver a convincing but subtle pitch to potential rebound guys, getting them into your court before you meet them.

✱ Fetch movies, ice cream, and the cute gourmet deli guy too.

## *The B Team*

Not every friend will make an all-star accomplice. In fact, some will make you feel worse than you already do, either because they aren't great friends to begin with or because they just don't have what it takes to help you through this situation. After the breakup, avoid friends and acquaintances that are part of the "B Team" (as in "Beware of these Bimbos").

* **The competitive friend:** She will be secretly happy you are in pain because she's always been a little bit jealous of you. She tries to compete with you in everything—your career, clothing, love life, and even your eating habits. She is a "one-upper." If you go to the gym three times a week, she goes five and teaches step aerobics. This girl will be thrilled to "help" you if you call her. She'll offer to talk to him for you and to buy you a lovely new outfit, like wooden clogs, lime green knee socks, and a floral Amish-style dress.

* **The quiet, genuine, insecure friend:** This girl is not your worst choice, but you might be doing her more harm than good by calling her. She'll try to understand, but she just won't get it. You can always meet another guy tomorrow. She can't even get her male boss to talk to her. Think of it this way—to her, you sound like the size zero in the dressing room who complains about her weight gain.

* **The friend who has a secret crush on your ex:** You know who she is—she calls him looking for you when she knows you're out of town. She e-mails him every morning just to say "hi." She's a little too close for comfort when you're out in a group. This friend clearly has ulterior motives. She'll be happy the two of you are having problems, but she'll also offer to help you win him back so she has an excuse to talk to him.

✳ **The friend who will expect a thousand favors in return:**
Once you open the floodgates, this girl never stops calling you.
She's needy. She has a major dramatic episode at least once a
day, so she will probably not understand the gravity of your
breakup. By asking for her help, you are opening yourself up
to a lifetime of phone-call dodging or long, inane conversations
if she catches you. Whatever cathartic cleansing you get from
her now will not be worth the endless favors you'll owe her in
the future.

✳ **The judgmental, self-righteous friend:** This girl is a nightmare with no sense of humor. She feels the need to dispense
her supreme advice even if you don't ask for it. If you tell her
you threw a beer in his face she rolls her eyes and says, "That
was not a very mature thing to do." Worse yet, she thinks
happy e-mail forwards about warm towels and spring flowers
are going to solve all your problems. Don't call her. The last
thing you need right now is someone telling you to see a
shrink just because you showed up at your ex's house with a
machete. Screw the shrink. Well, not literally—unless, of
course, he's cute and you have the necessary protection handy.

✳ **The friend who went through this "exact same thing":**
Beware of the friend who has good intentions but insists
"the same thing has happened to her before" so she knows

---

**Choose Your Accomplices Carefully**

Always ask yourself, "Do I like this person enough to
help her through a crisis down the road?" Regardless of
who you select, someday you will be *her* chosen accomplice and will be required to perform.

*To find out a girl's faults, praise her to her girl friends.*

*—Benjamin Franklin*

what you should and should not do, without question. You'll know who she is because she'll respond to every story you have with a story about herself and her own relationships. Listen to what she has to say and take from it whatever your rational mind tells you to take, but remember that no two relationships or breakups are alike. Ultimately, only you know what's best for you.

* **The married friend:** The married friend has good intentions, but 99 percent of the time a wedding snuffs out all the "single" brain cells. She'll agree to meet you for dinner or a drink but she'll be ready to go home by 10 P.M. You will want her to accompany you to the bar where he hangs out, but she won't remember where it is because she hasn't been out in five years. Your married friend will try to help you, and someday the two of you will see eye-to-eye again, but right now she is not living on your planet.

Don't feel bad about not choosing one of your B-team friends for this important mission. Focus on their good points, and then look elsewhere for your partner in crime. Do not try to convince yourself that you can get through the breakup without the support of a good friend. Finding a skilled and willing accomplice is critical to recovery. When it comes to coping with the post-breakup events, analyzing your ex's behavior, and discovering innovative ways to get back at him, two heads are better than one. Three heads are ideal, especially if the third one is his on a golden platter.

## Menacing Magic

If you haven't been able to make the jackass disappear using earthly tactics, try a little magic. A breakup isn't complete without the melodious sound of a devious spell sweetly chanted. Witchcraft, shrinking-head rituals, psychic practices, and other mystical solutions to guy problems make their way into breakup literature time and again. The idea of whipping up a potion and changing a man into a cute handbag is too appealing to ignore.

Unfortunately, there's not much evidence that any of this crap really works. Despite the millions of voodoo dolls made and sold, ex-boyfriends everywhere still have all their limbs. That's why it is important that as a diva, you take a more direct approach when practicing menacing magic. Jump to the wild side of hocus-pocus and integrate the following into your act.

### Dumping the Potion

Whip up a potion using all the necessary ingredients to make him disappear. Give it a few minutes to work, but don't wait forever. If you don't see results promptly, turn the burner on high, add in a few strongly scented spices, and then take the smelly, hot mixture and dump it directly over his head. Never wait for a force you can't see to do the job for you. Take it into your own hands and make sure it's done right.

### The Voodoo Slingshot

To make your own voodoo doll, grab a stone, stick it in the leg of a cut-off pair of pantyhose, tie your creation with a string just below the stone (to make the head), and draw a face on it.

Voila! Just in case the thing does work, it already has no arms or legs, so your job is half done. If it doesn't work fast enough for you, use the doll as a slingshot. Place the stone head in ready position and shoot your ex in the ass when he walks by.

### Shrinking Heads

Discover the age-old shrinking-head (or shrinking-wee) ritual. To find an expert in black magic to guide your experiment, you probably have to travel to an exotic location. However, do you really need to? Obviously, someone already tried and succeeded in the "wee" department. And his brain is so small, will shrinking his head even make a difference? Leave well enough alone, save your cash for a tropical vacation, and skip trying to inflict additional shrinking on a guy who is already the world's smallest man.

**A Sassy Spell**

While you're whipping up a gooey potion to make him disappear, find a spell or two for yourself to help you along the road to recovery. It's amazing what a little magic can do for the diva who believes. Here's a spell to get you started:

*Abracadabra, Abracadoo,*

*My ex is a loser and lame through and through,*

*Bring me a new hunk with brains and with girth,*

*Erase the old one from the face of the earth.*

## Fab and Furious

If you're feeling fab and furious, you've moved on to the next phase of recovery. At this point tears take a rest, and anger jumps in the fight for a round or two. Anger is a normal emotion for those who grieve-a like a diva. He shocked you with this breakup, and now continues to act like an ambiguous ass. Of course you're furious and dreaming of ways to release your frustration on him.

You'll know you've made the transition from sadness to anger when you start asking questions like these:

- Who the hell does he think he is, anyway?
- Why does the bastard assume he has the right to ask how I am?
- Why do law enforcement officers let men like him roam the streets?
- Would anyone notice if I put a "Ram Me. I'm an Asshole." bumper sticker on the back of his car?
- Is he still breathing, and is there a legal way I can stop it?

Remember the good old phrase "expressing your anger is healthy"—as if your anger is a tasty vitamin-packed granola bar? Anger is not healthy; it is akin to a chocolate-covered caramel brownie sundae with whipped cream and sprinkles. It is a

*Wickedness is a myth invented by good people to account for the curious attractiveness of others.*

*—Oscar Wilde*

delicious, irresistible treat and you deserve it right now—but if you have too much of it, you will get sick plus you'll have to lube your hips with baby oil to get your jeans on.

Anger is satisfying to a point, but it is important that you work through it so it doesn't consume too much of your time and energy. You need to spend most of your free moments rebuilding your life, making him jealous, and meeting new men. Anger will detract from these more productive objectives.

> You can get a great workout by making a punching bag of your ex. Just stuff some towels into a trash bag and stick a print-out of his face on one end. Or just find the real thing and go at it.
>
> Sassy Scoop

## *Anger Management for Darling Divas*

These steps will help you eliminate anger and move on to being fab and not-so-furious.

### Take the Colorful Path Through the Woods to Get to the Clearing

Sometimes the first step in getting anger out of your system is to indulge your creative revenge fantasies for a while. Though revenge schemes can be harsh and even illegal, you can often find ways to tone them down so they satisfy your urges without any grave consequences. Try the following:

**Fantasy:** Fly a skywriting plane above his barbecue. Spell out "die bastard" in white puffy smoke.
**Harmless version:** Etch "die bastard" on his lawn in the snow on a cold January morning.

**Fantasy:** Send his picture to local police with a note suggesting he is the assault suspect they've been searching for.
**Harmless version:** Send his picture to an online dating site and check off the "obese men over forty" box in preferences.

**Fantasy:** Bribe the exterminator to use hazardous bug bombs in his apartment without telling him.
**Harmless version:** Capture a disgusting bug, seal it in an envelope, and tape it to his door with a note signed "The Ex-Terminator."

**Fantasy:** Snip the chain behind his house with pliers and take his dog for a week or two.
**Harmless version:** Find fake fur that looks similar to his dog and tie the limp, lifeless piece to the chain.

**Fantasy:** Steal his newspaper on your way to work every morning.
**Harmless version:** Just take the sports section and use it as a coffee coaster.

**Fantasy:** Prank him all night long to keep him awake.
**Harmless version:** Program his number into a fax machine and let it do the work for you.

**Fantasy:** Bribe his six-year-old cousin to yell out "He hits me and it hurts" in earshot of authorities.
**Harmless version:** Have the spunky kid ask him if he swallowed a watermelon, poke him in the stomach, then run away.

If you suppress your anger, it is bound to come back even stronger down the road. So get through this angry phase by indulging some of your fantasies and perhaps even carrying out a

*When you plan to get even with someone, you are only letting that person continue to hurt you, but at least you get to hurt them too, and that's pretty satisfying.*

—*Anonymous*

few harmless maneuvers for amusement. Then you'll be ready to move on to step two in anger management for darling divas.

### Replace Anger with Humor

The second step in putting anger to rest is to begin to see your ex from a different, more humorous perspective. Realize that his pathetic behavior is actually laughable. Instead of letting it frustrate you, feel sorry for the loser. He is nothing more than a slug feasting on the lettuce leaf of life, and you are the human shoe getting closer and closer to squashing him.

Recall things he did that seem completely ridiculous in hindsight. They might include:

- Putting the lava lamp in the middle of the table as a "romantic" centerpiece.

**Sassy Scoop**

Do not be afraid your ex will remember you for years to come as the psycho girl he dated. He couldn't even remember your anniversary or what time he was supposed to arrive for your big date. Chances are he'll never be able to piece together memories of his harrowing times. Remember: Unless you do it naked, it is as good as gone when it hits his little brain.

- Asking you to comment on how much his arm muscles have grown from three trips to the gym.
- Calling you nicknames like "sweet pea" and "baby doll."
- Asking you to pick out clothes for him and then match up his stack of mismatched black and white socks.
- Inviting his old buddy "Doughboy" to join you for dinner on your anniversary.
- Wearing his favorite stained T-shirt to your parents' house.
- Busting out a suit from high school to wear to your cousin's wedding.
- Getting far too excited about *CHiPs* reruns.
- Drinking liquor out of the bottle when he thinks you're not looking.
- Leaving his smelly sneakers next to the room's air circulation system.
- Dancing like he's dodging falling meteorites.
- Snoring like he swallowed a live grizzly bear.
- Wrapping your holiday presents in shopping bags and thinking you won't notice.

Once you separate yourself from him and look at his behavior objectively, it will be next to impossible not to laugh. Your fury will be replaced with a feeling of amusement and tranquility.

*He told me I'm beautiful when I'm angry. Big mistake.*

*—Anita Liberty*

This new "calmer than Buddha" attitude will help you regain your footing faster than he can find the TV remote in a dark room. You'll be well on your way to the next phase of recovery, where your objective will be to focus on the fabulous you.

## A Targeted Plan for Every Lame Man

No matter what type of guy your ex is, there are plenty of ways to torment him. Use your time wisely. Craft plans that push your ex's personal buttons no matter what his lifestyle, and you'll feel much more satisfied with the results.

People will say "Don't break into his e-mail or prank him." But that's like saying "Don't eat the fresh chocolate chip cookie in your hand" and "Don't go to the bathroom after the eight-hour car ride." A diva's gotta do what a diva's gotta do. Instead of trying to quell your ingenious vengeful urges, practice them on the people who tell you to stop. After all, practice makes perfect, and your ex deserves nothing but your very best.

Sassy Scoop

- The Yuppie Ex: "Accidentally" erase his Palm Pilot . . . and the backup too.
- The Artistic Ex: Streak his favorite Picasso with a line or two of red finger-paint.
- The Jock Ex: Rub a little stinky, hot sports-injury cream into every jock strap he owns.
- The Mama's Boy Ex: Cut little holes in his footsie wootsie socks.
- The Commitment Phobic Ex: Sign him up for a monthly selection from an aggressive mail-order CD business.

- The Unemployed Ex: Remind him that he is jobless by sending him information about openings at sewage treatment plants nationwide.
- The Outdoorsy Ex: Help him get back in touch with nature by letting a tiny spider run free in his bed.
- The Redneck Ex: Smash his favorite Dale Earnhardt Jr. beer cooler.

**Let It Go**

When you start to feel better, cut down on the amount of breakup talk and analysis you do with your friends. Though it's important to hash out the relationship issues, there's no use in beating a dead ex.

# Chapter Four
# Look Sexy, Feel Fabulous

You've spent weeks, maybe months, reflecting on what happened and coming to terms with why things ended the way they did. You've finished crying, you're less angry than you used to be, and you're even enjoying your freedom. Now that your emotional healing is well under way, it's time to stop thinking about the breakup and focus again on your dazzling self. With a little enthusiasm and the right pair of heels, you'll have your star quality back in no time and he'll be groveling at your door.

## The Highway to Stardom

To be a sassy superstar, begin with your mind and turn yourself into a supremely self-confident being. Confidence is not something that happens to you. It doesn't stem from your circumstances in life, your looks, your success, or your wealth (not that a couple of million dollars ever hurt anyone). It begins with a conscious

*Nobody can make you feel inferior without your permission.*

*—Eleanor Roosevelt*

*But you can make your ex feel inferior without his.*

*—Sassy Diva*

effort on your part to live your life every day being true to your inner goddess, reminding yourself that you can handle anything that comes your way.

It will take a while to get your confidence back after a breakup. You can't expect it to happen overnight. Some days you'll find it easy to go out into the world and feel good about yourself. Other days you'll think life would be easier if you worked as one of those football mascots and could wear a mask and furry body suit all day. It's common to fluctuate back and forth between a "conquer the world" and "wear full fur garb" mentality, but the only way you'll ever get over the latter is to get out there and give the world another go.

The good news is that you can have complete control over your own feelings and thoughts even if you don't always feel like you do. You can start today to try to make total self-confidence a

**Sassy Scoop**

If you run into your ex before you feel ready to handle him, act as if you are completely over him. If he asks you how you forgot about him so easily, just for kicks, tell him, "I didn't. I'm practicing the 'Fake it till ya make it' philosophy. You know, the same one I used in the bedroom."

state of mind (a line taken right out of one of those cheesy self-help guides). Use the tried-and-true technique touted by motivational speakers everywhere: Even if you don't feel confident and fully recovered, act as if you do. As soon as you begin to think and act like the person you want to be, you become fully committed to moving in that direction. Before long, you will be that person. Just be careful. Don't inadvertently imagine yourself as a homeless woman or a 500-pound Deal-A-Meal candidate. You will become what you think about, and the last thing you need right now is Richard Simmons banging down your door in some skimpy spandex number.

### Ditch Perfect

The first step toward supreme self-confidence is to ditch the ridiculous notion that you can somehow be perfect. You might imagine that someday you'll have perfect thighs, the perfect job, or the perfect spouse. Life will fall into place and you won't have to work so hard. No difficulties or obstacles will appear, and you will be happy and able to rest. This state of problem-free living will happen, of course, when donkeys fly and hot men know how to cook.

The pursuit of perfection is endless and unachievable. First, it is a moving target dictated by the culture and the time in which we live. Even though you are probably very good at hitting moving targets by now (the damn bastard never sits still, does he?), perfection is one goal that is flat-out impossible to achieve.

The perfect woman at the turn of the twentieth century is not the perfect woman today, and the standard will never stop changing. In addition, what you think of as an imperfection might turn out to be one of your greatest assets. What happens if you need it sometime after you've eliminated it from your life?

For example, you might think it is bad to be sensitive, but think of how this quality will come in handy when you have to feign concern for your ex's skiing accident and hold back your laughter. Sensitivity is a great quality despite one of the all-time favorite male retorts: "You're too sensitive."

Study your own imperfections and think about how they might be useful. Maybe someone up there knows what you need more than you do. Instead of trying to fix yourself, try to learn to appreciate the unique things about you and put them to work for you in your life. Remember that your ex's imperfections are fatal flaws, but yours are assets in disguise.

### Top Ten Signs That Life Will Never Be Perfect

1. "Fat-free" foods still have trace grams of fat.
2. Price tags come off a new toilet brush with ease, but they stick like hell to fancy gifts.
3. The four-day work week has not even made it to the discussion phase in Congress.
4. The only sizes left on the sale rack are X-small and XX-small.
5. Even skinny women get cellulite.
6. Movie theaters actually sell tickets for the seats that require people to look straight up.
7. There's never anywhere to go on a good hair day.
8. Birthing rooms still lack devices that allow the husband to feel every contraction.
9. Almost every woman's current boyfriend is somebody's slimy ex.
10. Somewhere right now an atrocious man is smiling.

## *Visualize Outcomes*

Confident, successful people visualize their own success and happiness long before they have it. They actually see themselves in the place where they want to be instead of where they are. It is easy after a breakup to get stuck in one frame of mind. A negative thought can run in circles in your brain, appearing every morning just seconds after the alarm sounds and staying with you the entire day.

Post positive notes on your mirror to remind you of all the things you have to be happy about in life. "My friends are great, I have a clean bill of health, and I'm fertilizing the roses with my ex's ashes." Just remember to take them down before someone comes over to visit. You don't want to have to do any awkward explaining.

Sassy Scoop

### Visions of Happy Endings

As hard as it is to stop negative thoughts, make every effort to do so. The minute one pops into your mind, replace it with a positive thought like "He is not right for me. He is not worthy." Or concentrate on a motivating delightful vision like one of these:

- Imagine your ex contracting a rare form of incurable scabies.
- See yourself on an island being massaged with lotion by a chiseled sun god.
- Picture yourself winning awards and telling him to go to hell during your nationally televised acceptance speech.
- Envision him groveling at your feet in tighty whities in Times Square.
- Replace images of the perfect life with him and a golden retriever with more entertaining images of him locked behind a tall electric fence with a ballistic pit bull.

## Shrinky Dinks

You will not feel better all at once, but most divas do make steps toward recovery after the first month or so. If you feel profoundly sad and are unable to get any of your confidence and spunk back after two or three months, you might find that a long talk with a psychologist or psychiatrist is just the thing for you. Sassy divas everywhere are opting for psychiatrists. They can prescribe great drugs that can turn even the most depressed person into one of the annoyingly happy variety. But even if you are feeling better, it still may help to have someone objective to talk to about a situation.

### Healing Remedies

If you're still feeling blue but you're not quite ready to lie on a shrink's couch and pour out your problems, you can give natural remedies a try. There are lots of herbs and natural supplements that are said to have the ability to enhance mood and treat anxiety. Be sure to talk to your doctor before you take them, though. Some of these little gems are potent and they can interact with prescription and over-the-counter drugs. You don't want to grow hair on your chest. And make sure if you do take them, you buy a brand-name version—like designer shoes, label does connote quality in over-the-counter supplements.

*When you're away, I'm restless, lonely, wretched, bored, dejected; only here's the rub, my darling dear, I feel the same when you're near.*

—Samuel Hoffenstein

* **5-hydroxytryptophan (5-HTP):** 5-HTP is one of the building blocks of the neurotransmitter serotonin, the brain chemical that has been linked to a person's sense of calm and well-being. A protein-rich diet will yield adequate amounts of this amino acid; however, when ingested as protein, it competes with other amino acids in the body's absorption process. Nutritionists suggest that supplements are the way to go when you're trying to increase your intake of 5-HTP.

* **Saint John's wort:** This herb is touted as a natural form of Prozac, and some nutritionists do believe that it has a positive effect on mood. Saint John's wort affects the reuptake of serotonin in the brain. Many studies have been done on the effects of Saint John's wort, but they yield conflicting results. Nevertheless, it might be worth a try if you prefer herbal remedies to prescription medications.

* **Vitamin B:** Scientists have shown in countless studies that inadequate vitamin B in a diet contributes to depression and anxiety. Taking a multivitamin is a great way to guard against deficiencies of any type when you're going through a stressful period. Keep a bottle of adult chewables on your desk at work, and pop one after lunch. When you're through with the bottle, fill it with regular vitamins and offer a "chewable" to your ex.

* **Caffeine:** Caffeine offers a short-term pick-me-up because of its stimulating effects. Some studies have shown that those who suffer from depression find some reprieve if they consume a moderate amount of caffinated beverages each day. Obviously, too much caffeine can leave you jittery, anxious, and ready to run down your ex with a tank. But one tall latte a day can't hurt anything, and it might be just what the doctor ordered.

* **Carbohydrates:** Carbs are believed to have a calming affect on those who consume them because they provide the body with the building blocks necessary for the creation of serotonin. Some nutritionists theorize that people eat cookies, pastries, and bread when they are depressed because the carbs give them temporary relief. Though no one knows for sure whether or not this theory is true, go ahead and eat a few chocolate chip cookies every day during the breakup. Better safe than sorry.

* **Chocolate:** Proven to have a positive effect on mood, chocolate has sugar—a carbohydrate—and fat, which makes you feel satisfied. Nutritionists speculate that it has small amounts of the same mood-enhancing chemical found in marijuana. Others think the taste and experience alone are responsible for the pick-me-up. Regardless of the reason, give it a go. There are worse things than spending a few days snacking on chocolate everything.

Lots of options lie before you if you are looking for ways to enhance your emotional well-being. Research each option thoroughly, and go with the one that seems right for you. Most important, remember that anytime you feel depressed, someone or something is available to help you feel better again.

### Chocolate: The Perfect Breakup Food

Are you a person who has no appetite after a breakup? Chocolate is the ideal fix. It packs on calories and lifts your mood at the same time. Enjoy losing a few easy pounds, and then put an end to that nonsense with a case of fudge peanut butter bars. Buy wholesale for savings.

> *Researchers have discovered that chocolate produces some of the same reactions in the brain as marijuana. The researchers also discovered other similarities between the two but can't remember what they are.*
>
> —*Matt Lauer*

## Move & Groove

Once you're feeling confident and brilliant, get out there and put your best foot forward, clad in an A-List stylish heel. You can't find a new guy to make your ex jealous while sitting in your apartment sulking and plotting. You've gotta make a move. But before you think about beginning your search for Mr. Hot Rebound Man, prepare heartily for your grand re-entrance onto the scene. Stockpile the weapons you'll need to make a splash when you walk out the door.

Start with the most fundamental one of all: a healthy and radiant physique. While none of us can look like the airbrushed photos we see in the media, everyone can look and feel their best with a little movin' and groovin'. So get to the gym, turn up the Gloria Gaynor, and disco until you're shapely and sizzling.

### A Health Kick for You, A Couple of Kicks for Him

You can probably rattle off a hundred excuses not to join (or go to) a health club, but you know that a healthy, shapely body is an essential element in the ultimate diva package. So examine your excuses one by one. Most likely you'll find that they are really just fears that will go away quickly once you set foot in the door.

**Excuse:** I'll be sucked in by a treadmill or get caught under a large barbell.
**Reality:** Trainers walk around the gym and make sure none of the machines eat any of the members.

**Excuse:** The gym is too expensive.
**Reality:** Depending on where you live, a health club costs, at most, as much as a month's worth of slice-and-bake cookies. Once you pay for it, you'll feel motivated to go and get your money's worth.

**Excuse:** I'm too tired.
**Reality:** A good workout actually gives you more energy. Chase after your ex with a sharp object for several miles, and you'll feel revived.

**Excuse:** I don't have the time.
**Reality:** You only need to attend three times a week to reap the cardiovascular benefits, and once a week to check out the men.

**Excuse:** I don't have the right clothes. Everyone will be judging me.
**Reality:** Unless you are going to a Hollywood "see and be seen" club, a T-shirt, shorts, and good running shoes will definitely do the trick. No one will be judging you, because they are all too worried about what they look like.

*It's not enough to run only when chased.*

—*Anonymous*

*Top Ten Reasons to Join (and Go to) a Health Club*

1. Hot half-dressed guys everywhere, and you have a convenient excuse to talk to them. "Excuse me? Do you know where the sauna is?" Eventually one will offer to show you.
2. The gym offers karate classes and weight training. You will learn to fight your ex with ease and success.
3. If you work out on the treadmill, you will be able to run farther and faster. If he catches a glimpse of you stalking, you will be out of sight before he has a chance to identify your face.
4. You will acquire newfound confidence in your technical expertise from learning to operate the machines.
5. You will feel more confident after you've been attending for a few weeks and see other people come in with the "confused new member" look on their face.
6. You will quickly realize that several people in your neighborhood are in worse shape than you are (and they work out more often than you do).
7. Your cute clothes will fit better and you'll be able to wear new things you couldn't wear before.
8. If you aren't trying to lose weight, you will be able to eat more.
9. Working out for just thirty minutes, three times per week, improves mood, increases energy level, and boosts sex drive.
10. You've probably heard a study or two touting the health benefits of working out. That's probably an important thing to mention here. Aside from the cardiovascular benefits, aerobic exercise helps reduce and prevent varicose veins and cellulite. Weight training also reduces your risk of osteoporosis.

**Your Personal Best**
Don't fall into the trap of fighting the natural shape of your body or trying to conform to a picture that is computer generated in the first place. You won't look good if you are too thin or too buff in certain areas, and you'll only get frustrated if you try to turn yourself into the latest airbrushed cover model. Just work to enhance whatever you've been given, and you will look your best for years to come.

Still not convinced that a health club is right for you? That doesn't get you off the exercise hook. Many other options are calling your name. If you have the bucks, you can buy your own treadmill, elliptical machine, StairMaster, or weights (or go for it all!). Work out in the privacy of your own home with no creature looking at you except your cat. Or take to the trails, even if it's nothing more than a sidewalk with lots of streetlights. People always yield for joggers coming their way because no one wants to encounter a sweaty, moving entity by accident. If neither of these options appeal to you, throw on the Gloria Gaynor and do a cute little lip-synch disco number, alone (just make sure you close the blinds so your neighbors don't think you've gone nuts). Dancing to any uplifting song will burn calories, put you in an "I am a disco goddess" state of mind, and prepare you for future nights out on the dance floor.

Don't forget the little things that can burn lots of calories with minimal effort: take the stairs, walk to work, ride a bike, or creep up behind your ex and wrestle him to the ground. The key to being fit is to keep active, get your heart rate up, and build muscle. The key to losing weight is to burn more calories than you consume. Whatever your goal may be, get to work today on movin' and groovin' toward stardom.

### *Brownies and Diet Soda: The Fifth Food Group in the Nutrition Pyramid*

If you are truly going to outwit and outlive your ex, you need more than an active lifestyle. You also need to eat the right things for health and exuberance. Public service announcements broadcast the reasons you should eat a healthful diet—nutrients, energy, immunity from disease, and so on. However, most of us never pay attention to these messages, so we've spent years living on weird combinations of food like bagels and coffee or chocolate and Diet Coke.

If you can work some serious Internet surfing into your day at the office, you can learn quite a bit about the way your diet affects your memory, learning ability, mood, appearance, performance, and sex drive. Once you start reading about the benefits of eating different foods, you will probably become horribly frightened at first, because you'll realize that if you keep doing what you've been doing, you might die from scurvy or some other obscure disease caused by vitamin deficiencies. Then you'll feel motivated to expand your food choices to include everything your mother told you to eat. Help your ex along, too. Toss him a nice poison ivy salad.

**From the Diva Academy of Weights and Measures**
In addition to coming in handy when you want to punch his lights out, your fist doubles as a convenient device for measuring an appropriate serving size during meals.

Don't bother cutting out all junk food, buying special foods, or matching your intake to some obscure chart or meal plan. The only thing that really works is the "everything in moderation" principle. Tattoo that phrase on your hand, and follow it as if it's a divine law. (It's okay, though, to break down every once in a while, slip on a glove, and ignore that annoying little sucker.)

Some health nuts believe that you can select the right foods for a meal by making sure several colors are represented. Breads and meat are generally brown. Dairy products are yellow and white. Fruits and vegetables are multiple colors. If you follow that thinking, you can start your morning off with a heaping dish of rainbow sherbet and wash it down with a frozen slushy filled with colorful ice cubes.

*Sassy Scoop*

Pick up fruits and vegetables at the local deli. While there, bribe the owner to bury a long hair in your ex's sandwich. He deserves a delicious treat.

## Recipe
### Low-Calorie Healthy Smoothie

This recipe makes more than enough for one, so drink half and pour the rest over the junk that your ex never picked up—double the satisfaction, half the calories.

*½ banana*
*1 cup strawberries*
*Milk (as much as you like for desired consistency)*
*Handful of ice cubes*
*1 teaspoon sugar or honey*

Place ingredients in blender. Blend until smooth.

**The Most Important Meal of the Day**
Every morning, make yourself a big bowl of Bitch Flakes, the Breakfast of Champion Divas, for that little extra kick you need to make it through the day with sass. Serve him a prune cake with a cup of coffee, a chocolate-laxative muffin, or any variation of these two stomach-churning treats.

## The Beauty Queen Routine

Once you're feeling healthy and full of energy, you'll want to find a place to go dancing. Make sure it's filled with fun friends and enough cute men to go around. But don't go just yet. First make yourself even more dazzling by bringing your beauty routine up to snuff. You undoubtedly already know what it takes to be the star of any party, but review the steps again and make each one a little more fun and therapeutic.

Yoga can help you relax. Twist your ex's body into pretzel-like positions until he screams "uncle," and your tension will dissipate.

Sassy Scoop

Every recovering queen needs a "me" day to get her life back in order. A "me" day is a day to pamper yourself. You don't really want to say it that way, though. There's something kind of annoying about the word "pamper." It always conjures images of diapers, which in turn brings to mind all the immature men in the world. And though the term "me" day is not much better, it at least sounds a little selfish, which is exactly what the experience should be. So put on your best scratchy voice, call in sick, bring out the supplies, and carry out your beauty routine fit for a queen.

## Surefire "Me" Day Call-in-Sick Tactics

- Call right when you awaken, before sitting up, so your face is still scrunched into morning position and your voice sounds strained from lying down.
- Cover your mouth and cough up a little saliva to make it sound like you're hacking.
- Have a few mixed drinks the night before so your throat really is scratchy in the morning.
- Call from the street "on your way to the doctor," and then get cut off.
- Put a clothespin on your nose to fake a nasty head cold.

## A Fabulous "Me" Day

Prepare for your "me" day by sifting through your bathroom cabinet and getting out items you want to use in your beauty ritual. Sort through the thousands of tiny bottles, samples, creams, soaps, and weird fluffy scrubbers that have been rotting in there for years. If nothing looks useful, throw it all out and make room for new, good stuff. Once you have the space, you can even store your ex's old pictures beneath your tampons, where they belong.

If you are up for something a little new, take a trip to your favorite shop and try out a new facial cleanser or moisturizer. After all, you've finally gotten rid of the biggest zit you had in your life—him—so why not try to get rid of the rest? If switching products is not your style, you can spice up the standard "me" day procedures with a few of the following ideas.

### The Long, Hot Bath

Relax in a long, hot bath, but don't stay in it too long or you will turn into a tired, withered, floral-scented prune. You may not solve the world's problems relaxing in a bath, but you can have a little fun with voodoo and the like. The tub of water provides the perfect opportunity for you to play with the ex-boyfriend voodoo doll you made when you read Chapter 3. Hold it down with your feet while you drift off to relaxing music. Or light it on fire with the candle, then douse it quickly with bath water. When you're done with your bath, tie the voodoo doll to the drain and watch it try to bob up as the water whirls around.

### A New Haircut or Style

Right after a breakup, it is best to steer clear of drastic changes to your hair unless you are the naturally adventurous type. Why voluntarily make a bad situation even worse? If you really want to try something new, use a shampoo or conditioner that will give your hair a touch of color. If you typically wear your hair one way all the time, try changing it a little with over-the-counter products. A dot of funky gel can make it look sleek and sexy or curly and wispy. If you're determined to go for a cut, make a simple change to mark the beginning of a new, more positive era in your life. While you're out, stop by his hair place and bribe the barber to give him that stylish Daddy Warbucks look.

### Hair Removal

If you have unwanted hair, there are lots of options out there other than shaving. Over-the-counter creams and waxes work great. If you are afraid of waxing, try it on your ex first. Pick a really hairy spot on his body and pour on the hot wax. When it dries, rip it off very slowly.

To remove the hair from his furry body, grab a role of duct tape and press it to his leg firmly. Then when he least expects it, rip it off. If you're looking for something a little more subtle, Nair in his shampoo bottle will do the trick too.

Sassy Scoop

A basic Internet search will turn up thousands of articles on methods of hair removal. Research your options and choose wisely.

### Manicure/Pedicure

Every diva needs glistening toes and fingertips to match her fabulous dress and personality. If you don't want a stranger touching your feet, you can perform the rituals at home in the privacy of your own bathroom. Soak your hands and feet for ten minutes in warm, soapy water, push back your cuticles, and rub unsightly areas with a pumice stone. Send the stone to your ex and have him do his entire face. Maybe he can chisel down the size of his head a bit so it doesn't take up the entire room. After you're finished with the cleaning and scrubbing phase of your mani/pedi, toss on a colorful coat of polish that strikes your fancy. Then, go show off your toes in a sexy pair of strappy sandals.

### Full Body Massage

You can invest in a simple massage machine to have on hand at home, but why bother when Fabio is waiting at a salon to give you a full body rubdown? Many divas are wary of spending money on such extravagant beauty rituals, but that's because they don't realize how essential a massage is to health and peace of mind. A massage not only feels wonderful, it increases blood circulation and relieves tension buildup in every part of the body.

Get rid of your ex for good by giving him your own version of a full body rubdown. Walk on his back and forget to take off your cute Dolce and Gabbana spiked heels.

**Sassy Scoop**
Try a fantastic and therapeutic mud wrap. Trip your ex, wrestle him to a damp and marshy area, and then wrap away. You'll feel years younger.

### Sunshine in the Sky or in a Bottle

Tanning, in moderation, can be just the thing you need to brighten your mood and give you a healthy glow. If you opt for the real sun, wear full UVA/UVB protection when you're out there. Premature wrinkling is not on the diva to-do list. If your skin is too sensitive for the real sun, try an over-the-counter tanning spray or cream. Buy the well-known, reputable brand for yourself and a bottle of the cheap stuff for your ex, the soon-to-be orange-faced sucker.

### Beauty Rest

Remember to get plenty of sleep to round out your beauty routine. If you are still having trouble falling asleep at night because of the breakup, cut out caffeine after noon, try staying at a friend's place for a few nights, or take a nighttime cold medicine to help you doze off. If you have bizarre dreams, you might even learn some new ways to torment him that you never would have thought of in the waking world. Getting plenty of rest is essential for energy, motivation, and a positive outlook on life. Make sure you interrupt your ex's peaceful rest by having your friends in other time zones dial away.

### Drink Lots of Water with Your Martinis

Water is essential for your health, beauty, and energy level. It keeps your skin hydrated and your body in working order, and also helps to keep you awake and alert during the day. Mild dehydration is common, especially if you drink caffeinated beverages regularly and have a few alcoholic drinks now and then. If you feel irritable and tired, try drinking a glass or two and see if that clears it up. If not, your ex is the cause and you can dump the rest of the pitcher over his head the next time you see him.

Do everything you can to make yourself feel put together

**Don't Ever Forget . . .**
For every girl you see who seems to have it all together,
there is one looking at you thinking the same thing.

and ready to re-enter the scene. When you look your best, you'll
feel confident and radiant and you'll shine wherever you go.
Never let beauty rituals and routines fall by the wayside. They are
an important element in building your diva attitude.

### *Avoiding Beauty Accidents*

While enjoying a relaxing day to yourself, avoid the following
disasters that keep the hat and ski-mask companies in business:

- Going a little crazy with your facial and leaving marks
  that look like they were made by a skewer.
- Using new creams without checking for allergic reaction
  potential.
- Using special hair conditioners that leave your locks
  feeling like a grease ball.
- Becoming Lobster Diva by spending a full day in the
  sun with only cooking oil for protection.
- Overwaxing your eyebrows, leaving you looking permanently surprised.

### En Vogue Vixen

Clothes do not make the woman, but they sure do help. If you
look good and feel good in what you're wearing, you will emanate

*Clothes make the man. Naked people have little or no influence on society.*

—Mark Twain

attitude and command the respect you deserve as a superstar goddess. Go through your closet and get rid of the things you haven't worn in more than a year. Throw them out if they're grungy; donate them to a worthy cause if they're wearable. Even if it's the "special shirt you won during senior week," there is no sentimental value in an old dusty piece of material that has been stored in a box for years. Don't hold on to it unless you plan to frame it. Take a photo of it if you need to for your peace of mind, and keep that instead. Then toss it out and make room for the new pieces you are going to acquire that will be more appropriate for a sassy goddess.

## The Post-Breakup Shopping Spree

Once you've made room in your closet and drawers, set out for your favorite shops armed with cash and credit—preferably your ex's credit, but your own will do just fine. Unlike a regular shopping excursion, a post-breakup shopping spree is guilt-free. After all, you need the right outfit to re-enter the world in style, and nothing should stand in your way. Armed with your own good taste, pick out a sexy, classy ensemble that will make him grovel.

During a post-breakup shopping spree, cute shoes qualify as a "need" and not a "want." Pick up any pair with a heel. They'll make you appear taller and thinner and give him an instant height complex.

Sassy Scoop

Consider a few of these outfits:

* **Option #1:** Jeans, a fitted, short-sleeved shirt, and stylish shoes with a low heel. This combination says "I certainly didn't get dressed up for you, but I still look like a million dollars." This outfit will make you approachable to men everywhere while still giving you that chic edge. Casual, yet sexy, you can't go wrong with this denim classic.

* **Option #2:** A colorful wrap-around dress cut to the knee, and open-toed heels. This little number will make him realize what he's lost and make the other men in the room follow you like they're under hypnosis. Perfect for when you're ready to begin dating again, you'll catch any man's eye in this ensemble.

* **Option #3:** Black tailored slacks and a stylish, yet conservative top. Appropriate for when you're going out after work, this outfit will reek of class and sophistication. It will remind him that he'll be working for you before long and also enable you to get to know other men under the guise of business.

* **Option #4:** Fitted flared pants, a sexy top, and heels. Perfect for a Saturday night out when it's too chilly for a

*Shopping is a woman thing. It's a contact sport like football. Women enjoy the scrimmage, the noisy crowds, the danger of being trampled to death, and the ecstasy of the purchase.*

—Erma Bombeck

**Retail Growth**

Notice that your shopping mentality has changed. Whereas your ex was once better than the fabulous dress you found on the sale rack, now he's not even up to par with a great pair of thong underwear, nor nearly as thin.

skirt or dress, this outfit will make you the hit of any scene. Throw a jacket over the top to turn it into work attire. Take the jacket off at night for a stint of clubbing. This faithful ensemble is versatile and chic; throw it on, grab your club, and head for the door.

If you have trouble deciding on the right ensemble, bring along a friend. Some shoppers have a gift for picking out clothes and putting them together. Find the friend who can pick up a purple scarf, a leopard hair clip, and red leather pants, whip them together, and walk out of the house looking like a page out of *Vogue*. She will guide you toward your personal superstar garb.

The post-breakup shopping spree is also a perfect opportunity to pick up a few practical items to help you when you're stalking him, such as warm fleece, sunglasses, discreet headgear, and boots for navigating mountainous terrain. If he gave you his credit card and you still have it, don't forget to use it. Buy lingerie, a few unique bedroom toys, and a pick and a shovel, just to liven up his Visa statement. You can also make a stop at the local thrift shop to check out their funky retro items and, while you're there anyway, drop off a few of his things in exchange for a charitable tax deduction.

**Star Quality on a Budget**
You don't have to have a big bank account to look like a million dollars. In fact, a true goddess loves shopping in less expensive stores because she can buy several "will only wear once" pieces just for fun.

## Timeless Fashion Do's and No, Please Don'ts

When the dust has settled and you're back at your place sitting amidst a pile of clothes, don't be overwhelmed by the choices before you. With your great taste and attitude, you will look good in any star garb you choose. The general rule of haute couture is "if you feel good in it, you'll look great in it." Just abide by the classic do's and don'ts of fashion and then let your own creative flair show.

You probably know most of the "do's and don'ts" already, but if not, review them here.

**DO:** Wear comfortable shoes. You don't want to end up limping home three hours early on a Saturday night. Don't go overboard and buy orthopedic flats in every color, but do buy shoes that are reasonably comfortable so you can dance all night or run like hell after you dump a drink on your ex.
**NO, PLEASE DON'T:** Wear socks or pantyhose with your open-toed shoes. Nothing is less attractive than beige toes sticking out of summer sandals. Ditch the pantyhose and show off your sexy legs during the summer.

**DO:** Wear fitted clothing. Baggy clothes often make women look dumpy and heavier than they are. You never want to look like you're wearing a belted nightgown or an ex–football player's warmup suit. If you think you look fat in fitted clothing, wear dark colors. Black is always in, and it makes every woman look chic and sexy. Fitted black pants look good on everyone, fat and thin, short and tall, except your ex, of course. He only looks good when he's wearing a jailbird suit, a pair of handcuffs, and a bag over his head.

**NO, PLEASE DON'T:** Wear clothes that are so tight you can't breathe and need to be rushed to the hospital midway through the night. Men might ogle a woman dressed in suffocating spandex, but not for the right reasons. Ultratight clothing is a big no-no for work, but even on the weekend think twice before squeezing into a tourniquet dress.

**DO:** Wear interesting color combinations and clothing with a unique flair. You don't want to overdo it with bright tropical patterns, but color, at least around your face, will make you look vibrant. Go through your clothes frequently. Move the shirts in colors you haven't worn recently to the front of the closet, and then move the "old faithfuls" to the back so you don't get stuck wearing the same thing every week for a year.

**NO, PLEASE DON'T:** Pick out a color and then match your top and bottom. Glaring examples of this mistake are a denim jacket and mini (the "denim suit"), or a green pair of pants and matching green shirt ("the jelly bean look"). Leave the uniforms for the military, and opt for an ensemble with variety.

**DO:** Take a risk in your style and try something new. If you see a woman walking down the street and she looks great, note what she's wearing and give it a go. You might feel awkward at first if you try on flared dress pants and a conservative top and you're used to straight-legged jeans and lace. But give it a chance—a change can give you an entirely new outlook on yourself and the world.

**NO, PLEASE DON'T:** Wear embroidered tops, holiday-themed sweaters, or anything with bells or tassels hanging off it. If you aren't sure what to steer clear of in this category, take a trip to a casino and watch people for the day. Unless you are a cute little grandma or Dolly Parton in concert, ditch the tassels, large jewels, and embroidery, and go with something a little less busy.

**DO:** Wear accessories that complement your clothing—a simple watch, a cute bag, and a necklace in gold or silver. A string of pearls, funky beads, or a chain can rev up a work or evening outfit. Match your bracelet and earrings or keep them classic, and they'll go with anything. Experiment with scarves, hats, and other extras if you want to achieve a look that's a little different.

**NO, PLEASE DON'T:** Wear multiple chains and bracelets so you set off every metal detector in the country. Keep jewelry simple and accessories at bay. Just like men, they should not make or break the diva. They should simply enhance her. If you are wearing lots of chains, it might not be the breakup that's weighing you down. Take off those shackles and use them to whip him into shape.

---

### Keep Your Tootsies Happy

To make your shoes more comfortable, line them with insoles. If the shoes are open, cut the insoles into smaller pieces and position a piece under each foot where they won't show. Stick them in place with a dot of glue. No one will know they are there, and you will double the time you can wear your shoes before your feet need a rest.

**Fashion Flinch**
Pumps with jeans, feathered hair, and bright blue eye shadow are still hallmarks of the early 1980s. Don't bring them back before their time is due.

Other fashion faux pas include visors, fanny packs, visible panty line, shirts or jackets covered with animal pictures, pumps with shorts, and long fingernails with shapes and designs (unless you're in middle school). Of course, there are exceptions to every rule. A crazy party might be the right time to whip out the fake tattoo and nail sequins, but remember that these types of items always have their place. Dress like a diva and wear what makes you feel great, but guard against the fashion blunders that will detract from your stardom.

Remember that you are looking sexy and feeling fabulous for you, not for your friends, not for a guy, and not for people on the street. You are focusing on yourself so you feel good and have the confidence you need to live your life in any way you wish. That doesn't mean you are above watching your ex grovel. No one would miss out on such fun. What it does mean, however, is that you are focused on making yourself and your world the best it can be without a guy in it, and the first step in the process is to get your own mind and body in tip-top condition.

*Give a girl the right shoes and she'll conquer the world.*

—Bette Midler

## Chapter Five
# Be a Social Starlet

Your star quality is back and it's time to show it off. Muster all your enthusiasm and energy and book the busiest social schedule you've ever had in your life. Even if you don't feel 100 percent prepared to get back out on the social scene and start living again, you are as ready as you'll ever be. Get moving. With the right attitude and your social calendar in hand, you'll have more fun now than you ever did with him by your side.

### Rally the Glam Posse

To enter the social world with sparkling splash, you will need to rally a posse of glamorous female friends and get them riled up for a night on the town. Locate old phone numbers or e-mail addresses, find out what's going on around you, and get ready to book your calendar solid for at least the next few months. Feel ready? Great. Take a deep breath and prepare to run a social marathon in sexy heels.

A glam posse is a group of fun, confident women with an

*If everything seems under control, you're just not going fast enough.*

—Mario Andretti

insatiable appetite for pink boas and frozen margaritas. They are exactly what you need by your side when you step back out on the social scene. Rallying the glam posse will not be hard. Ideally you have friends you can contact who you used to hang out with before you met your ex. If these girls are worthy posse members, they will be thrilled to hear from their long-lost, newly single starlet pal.

If by chance you don't have too many good female buds around, whether it's because you've moved to a new city, lost touch with old friends, or they all got married, get to work on meeting a new, fun group of wing women to accompany you to social venues. True, it can be next to impossible to make new female friends once you're out of school. After all, you can't exactly go up to a girl in a bar and ask her to hang out. But there are always ways to find glam posse members if you're willing to make a little effort.

* **Be proactive.** When you meet a potential gal pal, be the one who talks first. Ask her to hang out, or throw a party at your place and invite her. Chances are she is in the same position you are, and will be happy to make new friends.

* **Play the "I just moved here" game.** If you're self-conscious about telling people you just went through a breakup, tell them you're new to the area. Eventually, when they are full-fledged posse members, you can tell them the truth and put them to work with the rest of your ruin-his-life cheerleaders.

✱ **Seek out the enthusiastic nice person.** Wherever you are, look for the type of girl who is extraordinarily outgoing and introduce yourself. If you give her the "I just moved here" line, she'll probably give you so many e-mail addresses you won't know what to do with them all.

✱ **Join a networking group.** This is a great way to meet new people. Get involved with one through your career or alma mater. You don't have to like the activities or all the people. You only have to participate long enough to make a few friends. Of course, you never know—you might meet a new guy, too.

✱ **Attend dating seminars.** Dozens of women flock to seminars on relationship and dating issues. Look up seminars online, and attend one. You can ask around afterward and find out what people do on the weekends for fun. You'll meet women who are in the same situation you are, and many of them will probably have new, innovative ideas for tormenting an ex. You might learn something from the seminar, too.

Do whatever you need to do to meet new recruits for your glam posse. Good female friends are vital to your recovery. They

**Let Divas Eat Cake**
To spice up a "girls night in," invite your glam posse over for dessert. Take your ex's photo to the bakery and have them turn it into an edible image on the top of a cake. Give each girl a knife so she can slice a piece. You cut the first one of course, right through the middle of his head.

are fun and supportive and they'll share with you those moments and experiences that only women can understand. When you have good female friends around, dating will seem a little less important, and your shared stories will add an element of humor to the social scene.

You can always count on your glam posse to:

- Give new meaning to the phrase "divide and conquer" when they split up in a bar and find ways to torment your ex from every corner of the room.
- Make you feel popular on those days when you're feeling lame.
- Hold the bathroom door closed when the lock is broken.
- Ensure that you have at least one friend in town at all times who wants to go out and have fun.
- Be outrageous vacation buddies and car-trip companions.
- Help you network in your rise to power.
- Accompany you to chick flicks, girly events, and painful obligatory work parties.
- Contribute ideas to your revenge strategy that reflect their individual strengths.
- Celebrate your birthday, holidays, and all the good times by organizing a glitzy, star-studded affair.

It's easy to think that an active social life comes naturally, but the reality is that maintaining a social life is hard work. You have to go out sometimes when you don't feel like it, make the effort to keep in touch with people, and show an interest in others. The effort, however, is well worth it. By being active, you'll fill your life with fun, friends, and the energy you need to be the dynamic diva you were born to be.

### Hello, I'm . . .

Never avoid meeting new people because you are afraid to make small talk. Though it can be uncomfortable to chitchat with a random person, it can't possibly be as painful as the conversations you've had with your ex. If small talk is not your forte, keep a few questions on the tip of your tongue to ask whenever you experience an awkward silence:

- Where did you find that fantastic necklace?
- Who else is coming to the party?
- If you were moving, which part of this city would you move to? Or would you jump ship and go cross-country?

Steer away from questions like:

- What is that large, black dot on your cheek?
- Oh, I love that shirt! But don't you feel like it looks a little tacky on?
- Have you put on weight since the last time I saw you?

If the conversation takes a turn for the worse, excuse yourself to go to the bathroom, make a phone call, or grab a much-needed drink at the bar.

## Priorities on the Scene

You look fantastic and you and your glam posse are poised to have the time of your life. You're prepared to handle anything that comes your way. As you dance out the door with your boa trailing behind you, keep these tips in mind. They'll ensure that the night will be a big success.

### Have a Good Time

Make an effort to enjoy yourself and keep the evening light and amusing, even if it means having fun at your ex's expense. Play games in the bar and get people talking. Watch the guys walking by and give them nicknames based on an outstanding physical feature. Play "How many men will buy drinks for me and my posse?" It's a game that's good for you and your bank account too.

### Keep an Eye Out for the Ideal Rebound Man

Even one that's not so ideal will do the trick. Heck, there are plenty of cute himbos out there. Find one to take advantage of. You'll feel much better once you kiss a hunky new guy. You don't want to miss him while he's walking by, so keep diligent watch.

### Do Not Search for Your Ex

If you go to a bar or a party and he's not there, don't leave to drive by his house or perch on a fire escape outside his window. You might not be prepared to tell him off yet, so a divine force is keeping him out of your path. If you can't suppress the urge to look for him, at least be discreet. You want any future run-in to seem totally unplanned so you can ask him if he's stalking you, pre-empting any insinuation he might make that you're the one doing the stalking.

### Request Upbeat Tunes

Don't spend the evening in Discuss the Breakup (DTB) mode. Request some fun, fast songs, and have a good time. You

*A drink a day keeps the shrink away.*
*—Edward Abbey*

**Ex-cellent Advice**

"No pain, no gain," is a great phrase to use when your ex asks you why you're trying to hurt him with a dull steak knife, but it is also a great phrase to keep in mind yourself when you're doing something that's difficult but good for you in the long run.

need a break from plotting his demise so you can return to it with a new perspective and fresh, creative ideas. So crank up the cheesy tunes, drink something fruity out of a fishbowl, and get out on the dance floor.

Keep these priorities in your mind when you're out, and stick to them faithfully. They will help you acclimate to the scene again. Once you do, everything will fall into place, meaning you'll feel awesome, your ex will seem far worse than you ever imagined, and you'll be happy that you're moving on to bigger and better things.

## Mingle Mania

Once you have the priorities of the evening in order, you and your glam posse are ready to step out onto the red carpet and enjoy the scene. Post-breakup mingling is a very special kind that will let you bask in the limelight and recall the days before you met him, when life was simply grand. Whether you're a party person or a bar babe, your job is the same: grab your cutest handbag, pack it for the occasion, and get out the door rain or shine, snow or hail, thin or fat—just get out there. The scene might not look exactly like it did the last time you were living it up as a solo celebrity, but you'll get your groove back in no time.

## So Many Options, So Little Time

The social options are endless and sometimes your calendar will be overwhelming, but if you stick to a few basic principles, the entire glam posse will have a fabulous time, guaranteed.

First, when you think about options for parties, new friendships, or places to go, always consider enhancing your social life while detracting from his. Remain good friends with his guy friends or his siblings. Throw parties and invite everyone he knows. It's okay to mingle like crazy and exact revenge at the same time.

Next, avoid places and things that are "heinous by association." If there is one place you and your ex always frequented, there's no need to go there now. If you are going to walk back and be flooded with memories of him scarfing up a hamburger or drinking dozens of dollar drafts, go elsewhere. Trade off these places—for new, more spectacular venues.

However, do not stay home completely out of fear that you might run into him or be reminded of him. Even though you are avoiding places that are heinous by association, that doesn't mean you should stay inside shored up in solitude, or miss the most fabulous party of the century because there's a slim chance he might show up. Do not give him enough power over your life to turn you into a hermit.

Remember to keep it upbeat—only frequent those places with a good vibe and lots of people. The bar described in nightlife guides as "a scene from *Night of the Living Dead*" would not be the ideal post-breakup pick. The glam posse is

*I met a guy out on Saturday night, but he had to go home to brush his tooth.*

—Anonymous Diva Who Frequented Dive Bars

probably fab enough to know that only the fun, upbeat places are worth an appearance, but pay close attention to the group's picks just to make sure that the social venues remain appropriate for high-caliber sassy divas.

As you explore your party options, keep places that have a decent-sized bathroom on the top of your list. Finding a good bathroom is the bane of every social starlet's existence. What is merely a minor inconvenience on a regular night out can be a major problem after a breakup. A bathroom provides a fantastic place to congregate away from the madding crowds. You'll need a stall to hide in if you see him, or to cry in if you run into him and he's acting like a huge jackass toward you. You'll need mirror access to make sure you're looking fab at every moment you're circulating. So avoid places with a Porta Potti, and go for the fifteen-stall paradise.

Once you are out, don't hide in a corner with the posse or form the "circle of death." The circle of death is a tight-knit group of divas that resembles a fuzzy pink blob from afar. Its closed-off appearance often prevents others from penetrating the ring and mingling with the posse. Mingling, after all, is the whole point of the evening.

Finally, if you live in one of those locations where there's nothing more than a corner bar, a stoplight, and a grocery store—and the store is the most appealing weekend hangout—

take drastic action. Grab your glam posse and drag them to the closest big city at least once a month. Try to get a job in a nearby area or take some classes in another town so you're forced to leave the boundaries of your locale. Do whatever it takes to expand your options and mingle with people near and far.

### Party On

A good glam posse can throw fun, glitzy theme parties that will enhance any social life. Among the possibilities:

- Seasonal parties, like a summer fling with Hawaiian shirts or a festive party with holiday garb.
- A glam posse bonding party where members make T-shirts that share a common slogan, like "Fun & Fabulous."
- A revenge party where each girl writes the name of her ex(es) on the specially made ex-boyfriend papier-mâché sculpture, and then partakes in a classic posse ritual of bringing the statue down with kicks and funky dance moves.

These types of events bring the glam posse closer together and build a unified social front.

### Top Groups of Guys for Glam Posse Mingling

Not just any group of guys is appropriate for post-breakup mingling. Be sure to stick with those that add to the festive mood. Though any group of adoring men can enhance the posse's social experience, the top groups worth interacting with after a breakup include:

### Guys from Out of Town

Adoring, cute, and confident men you never have to see again almost seem too good to be true when you're looking for a fun night with no commitment. Guys can be a drag when they always want to call and bug you days later. On a night when you just want to live it up, guys who will disappear after twenty-four hours or less are like a divine gift from the posse fairy godmother.

### Tolerably Nerdy Guys

Extremely nerdy guys can turn a fun glam posse into a group of fugitives, but a tolerably nerdy crew can be a most phenomenal post-breakup ego booster. These guys will look at the glam posse and see celebrities they are fortunate to have the opportunity to talk to. Their adoring gazes and attentive conversation will shine in contrast to the thoughtless, bumbling mentality of your ex.

### Gay Guys

If you want to learn a bitchy maneuver or two, surround yourself with gay men, a glam posse all-time favorite. You can't go wrong with a group of hunky men who look straight from afar but are as gay as can be. They will teach the posse a few beauty tricks as well as some sassy moves never before known by the diva community. They are outstanding partners in crime for a night on the town. Seek them out and buy them all a drink.

### Funny Guys

Guys with a sense of humor are an obvious glam posse favorite. They will bring a standup act to any festive social scene. Listen for jokes you can use at the expense of your ex. Every good glam posse needs a private night of comedy to spice up their calendar, so find the funny guys and go out for drinks.

### Off-Duty Bartenders and Chefs

Men with advanced knowledge of drinks, food, and social customs are excellent post-breakup social companions. They will bring the posse pink drinks you never knew existed. These guys can whip together an omelet when they don't even have eggs. They'll also help posse members bypass the line at the bar and make it to the front for VIP treatment.

### The Wealthy Crew

Even though the group of wealthy guys might be intolerable most of the time, your glam posse should be ready to reel them in during the month after the breakup. A night on a yacht with free drinks, hors d'oeuvres, and new social contacts is exactly what you and your posse need. While there, try to get them to fund your start-up revenge operation.

## Close Encounters

You know the minute you set foot out the door with no makeup on and your hair in a ponytail, he will come waltzing down the street escorting the female model his company is using for their marketing materials. Be prepared for this run-in. Whether you're going to parties, bars, or low-key dinner parties, at some point you'll be shocked all to hell because you'll turn a corner and there he'll be with that dumb look on his face. Maybe you'll look great, it will go smoothly, and he'll drop to the floor to worship you. However, it is important to imagine the worst so you'll be ready for whatever happens. Mental preparation is half the battle in coping with a run-in. Picture him kissing the girl you hate most right in front of you at a party. To make the image a little easier to bear, also picture him finding out he's contracted a rare lip disease a few weeks later. That situation will probably never happen, but if you prepare for the worst, you will be very pleased when he's at the party alone sulking by the cheese dip.

## Critical Preparations

Many people will tell you to avoid places where he's likely to be for a few months after the breakup. Of course, you won't. Any girl in her right mind would show up where he is on purpose just to bug him. But don't even consider risking a run-in without making a few preparations.

### Look Awesome

In addition to your already fabulous outfit, throw on heels and a little body glitter. If you tower a few inches above him, he'll feel like a short loser. The glitter will distract him so he doesn't notice the "holy shit" look on your face.

### Pack Your Handbag Accordingly

Bring tissues, your eye makeup, and eye drops just in case you cry. Also, throw in a box of allergy medicine with a huge label so you can pull it out in front of him and say "damn that pollen" when you start to get teary. Pack a mirror compact so you can whip it out to apply your lipstick and see what's happening behind you on the other side of the room. Throw in your cell phone so you can make a quick call to friends, family, or authorities if he does something extraordinarily horrific. Finally, always have an emergency tampon available. Murphy's Law states that on the night you run into him you will also get your period.

### Brief Your Friends

Tell them to support you without seeming obvious. A good friend will throw in random facts about your great life, a trip you're taking, an award you've won, or how you've been crowned princess of an influential tropical island. A good friend will also end the conversation between you and your ex by saying, "Come on. We're going to be late. Dave and Tom expected us ten minutes ago." If your friends are clueless and lack cunning, just tell them to keep quiet or offer them a fashionable Burberry muzzle.

### Know Your Alcohol Limits

When you see him, you might make a quick dart for the bar without even realizing it. Alcohol is a great way to cushion the blow and block out his irritating voice. If you can handle your liquor and have not had any bad experiences with it in the past, drink away. But if you have a history of throwing up easily and waking up in your bathtub face down, go easy on the drinking when your ex is around. Alcohol is a depressant, so something he says that might not affect you when you're sober can send you into a tearful rage when you're drunk. You don't want to hurt him in public with all of those witnesses around, so lay off the alcohol until he's gone or until they're gone—preferably the latter.

### Enlist the Help of Other Men

If you are going to a party, bar, or event and you know your ex will be there, bring another guy with you as a security blanket.

---

**The Three Ds**

Never drink and drive, drink and discuss, or drink and dial. Try to stay sober for your run-in so your actions are deliberate and your words are piercing. Of course, if a little alcohol makes you more sassy, it's okay to have a martini or two, but no more. Make him feel like a weasel—take a cab home.

If you don't have a few readily available just yet, invite a foreign student or college alumnus who just moved to your area, call a friend's brother or cousin, or ask one of your straight-looking gay pals to go with you. When you enter into this battle, no defense is better than a human shield of hunky men.

### Don't Assume an Ex-Sighting Is a Sign of Destiny

It could just be a divine sign that you need to tell him off in order to move on. Don't read meaning into something where there might not be any. Remember how poorly he treated you at the end of the relationship, and how great you're doing without him.

Exception: If he initiates contact, apologizes for his behavior, brings you flowers, chocolate, and something cool like an expensive digital camera, writes you a poem, begs your forgiveness on one knee, *and* flies you to a tropical resort with five-star accommodations, you can think about it.

> If you see your ex in a bar, pay the bartender to water down his drink repeatedly.
>
> Sassy Scoop

### Prepare to Fight the Green Gremlin

Jealousy is a natural feeling to have after a breakup, but it doesn't have to set you back in the recovery process. Remember that almost 100 percent of the time the scenarios you imagine are far worse than they actually are. If you are certain he is dating someone new, or that a girl he's talking to is the girl of his dreams, your mind is playing typical post-breakup tricks on you. Remind yourself that he is a big oaf and it will take him years to find someone who really likes him if he doesn't change his annoying ways. Find consolation in knowing that you can make him jealous too, simply by being your fabulous self, having a great time with your glam posse, and sending out a far-reaching "I'm over you" vibe. Even the most rock-solid guy will be slightly annoyed that you've moved on so quickly. So get to it.

### Plan Your Speech

Finally and most important, think about what you want to say and what you do not want to say when you speak to him again. You definitely will not stick to a plan

*Jealousy is all the fun you think they had.*

—Erica Jong

you establish now, but it is still good to have something on the tip of your tongue so you don't miss out on a golden opportunity to make him squirm. The last thing you want to do is blurt out something you want to take back right before he moves to Siberia for five years. Make the moment count. Have a little something up your sleeve—a razor-sharp ice pick, at the very least.

### *Keeping on Task*

A run-in is not a time to let the post-breakup blues work their way back into your head. You are a diva and you must keep on task. You have been given the opportunity to see him again, so milk it for what it's worth. Regain the upper hand, try to get closure, and

*I hate to advocate drugs, alcohol, violence, or insanity to anyone, but they've always worked for me.*

—Hunter S. Thompson

*When life gives you lemons, make lemonade. Add salt instead of sugar and pass him a tall, cool, refreshing glass.*

*—Anonymous*

at the very least, leave with a few good pieces of information you can use to torment him down the road.

### Regain the Upper Hand

To regain the upper hand, try to send the "I really couldn't care less if you live or die" message his way. When you run into him, always say you're doing great and feel fabulous even if it's not exactly true just yet. Don't give him the satisfaction of knowing you still care. The goal is to leave him more uncomfortable than he was before he ran into you, so turn on your demolition diva attitude and go to work. If you break down and tell him you miss him, the only way to salvage things is to latch onto him and scream "please don't go" so he's humiliated in front of everyone he knows. Given that this move would scare off good rebound guys, it is not the best option. Stay on task and tell him you're doing great. If you aren't yet sure that you can pull of the "I don't care" vibe, just pretend you don't see him. Spend the night dancing with a better guy, preferably someone he hates.

### Understand the Closure Process

Getting closure is a process in which two people discuss what went wrong in the relationship and learn where they stand with one another so they can move on. It is very difficult to erase all thoughts and lingering questions until you reach a point

> **Teletherapy**
> Think your run-in was a disaster? Watch a daytime talk show like *Jerry Springer* for a quick infusion of "Maybe things in my life aren't so awful after all."

where you just don't care about him anymore. Typically, you reach closure months after the breakup, when a change of circumstances gives the entire thing a sense of finality. You might see him again and notice he's changed dramatically, or you start dating a new guy you like better, or you grow in a different direction, look at your ex, and can't figure out what the two of you once had in common. Until one of these events occurs, use a run-in to evaluate where you are on the closure spectrum. The closer you get to full closure, the less effect a run-in will have on your state of mind.

# Evaluation
## The Closure Spectrum

With a rating of ten meaning "full closure" and zero meaning "none whatsoever," use this scale to evaluate how close you are to that sense of completion.

You see him and:

✱ **You run up to him and start crying.** He takes you outside to rehash the issues from the breakup—again. You take a cab home, sobbing hysterically, and refuse to venture out for a month for fear you'll run into him. *Closure rating: 0 or less*

✱ **A member of the glam posse handcuffs him and takes him outside for questioning while you make a getaway to**

**the bathroom to contain your tears.** After you've regained your composure, the two of you quiz him to try to figure out why he ended things and what his intentions are now. *Closure rating: 1–3*

✳ **You manage to have a civilized conversation with him, but afterward you can't stop thinking about him, analyzing his every word, and crying sporadically.** The rest of the night and the entire next week you and your friends discuss the meaning of the run-in. *Closure rating: 4–6*

✳ **You see him and you are unbelievably sassy.** A little piece of you is still annoyed that he had the nerve to break up with you, but generally you can see how wrong the whole thing was anyway, because he is obviously so far beneath you. This becomes grossly apparent when you watch him attempting to tread water in a sea of men who are better than he is. *Closure rating: 7–9*

✳ **You never even realize he is in the same room you are.** A week later, you're on the phone with a friend and she mentions to you that he was there. You half hear her, but you have to hang up because your favorite show is on. *Closure rating: 10+*

### Snag Useful Tidbits

Try to walk away from the run-in with a few really good tidbits of information you can use in the future to torment him. To do so, ask him questions about his life. Then you can respond to his stories with sympathy and an appropriate action down the road. For example:

> **Sympathy:** It's awful to hear about the alligator attack, but it's great they found your arm in the pond.
> **New battle plan move:** Buy him a pair of gloves for his birthday.

**Sympathy:** How terrible someone sent those naked pictures of you to your grandmother. I'm so sorry she died.
**New battle plan move:** Send the same pictures to his mother.

**Sympathy:** Wow. I'm so sorry to hear that bus dragged you until your bare feet were scraping against the pavement.
**New battle plan move:** Send him a gift certificate for a pedicure for men.

**Sympathy:** Your friends are really all moving away? I'm sorry. I know how hard that will be for you.
**New battle plan move:** Let your gay buddies know he's cold and lonely. Ask them to call him and have some fun with his homophobia.

## The Rumor Mill

The social scene is full of cute men, good gal pals . . . and also worthless slugs, rumor mongers, and other generally bothersome people and situations. While you're out being fun and fabulous, your ex isn't the only annoyance that can bring back unpleasant breakup feelings. Be prepared for other pesky people so you can handle them smoothly, even after a few martinis.

### Self-Esteem Secret
You might look around the bar and see other women laughing, smiling, and flirting as if they've never had a bad breakup in their lives. Remember that you look that way most of the time too. Other women do not possess some special secret gift for dealing with men.

## Prying Questions

Because you've gone through a breakup, you are an attractive target for gossips everywhere. Be flattered that they are so interested in your life, and then arm yourself with some sassy comebacks.

**Question:** When did you break up?
**Comeback:** We were never really dating. He was just using me as a cover because he's closet gay.

**Question:** What happened between the two of you?
**Comeback:** I'm glad you asked, because now I know it's really going to bug you if I don't tell you.

**Question:** Is it true he was cheating on you with _____ (insert name of local tramp)?
**Comeback:** I don't know, but as soon as his STD results come back, I'll let you know.

**Question:** Do you still love him?
**Comeback:** I never loved him. I was just using him for sex (or money, free Internet access, etc.).

When annoying questions come your way, counter them with sassy responses or little white lies. The one exception to this rule is a mutual friend of you and your ex. Handle her with kid gloves, as anything you say could make it back to him. No matter what the actual circumstances are, let her know you are doing great and feeling incredible.

Keep a few verbal punches on hand so you can respond to what can be the most annoying and condescending question of all: Are you okay? Try one of these sassy comebacks:

- Go to hell.
- Okay at what? I'm fabulous at everything.
- I was until I saw your face.
- Get your own life, you prying, gossipy scumbag.

### Rampant Rumors

Rumors are another story. They'll make it back to you, but you won't even know where they originated. If you can, find humor in the rumors that come your way and write them down so you can laugh at them with your friends. These are some of the things you might hear:

- She went psycho when he broke the news.
- She was with *300* guys before him.
- He tried to break up with her last year and she bashed the hood of his car in with a crowbar.
- She begged him to marry her and he wouldn't say yes.
- He's dating Miss Hawaii and Miss California at the same time.

If you encounter a person who says, "You are both nice people. You just weren't right for each other," answer them by saying, "Actually, he really sucks." You'll feel great that you stood up for yourself. Now is not the time to be singing his praises.

**Sassy Scoop**

The best way to handle these rumors is to laugh at them. If you wish, you can embellish them with ridiculous details just for amusement. Whatever you do, never argue with those who perpetuate rumors, because they don't even care if the buzz is true. They just want something to talk about. The more you appear to care, the more exciting it is for them.

Being social again is one of the most important steps in a diva recovery plan. Don't dive in unprepared, however. Rally your posse and know what pitfalls await the newly single goddess. When you do have all your battle plans in line, step out onto that red carpet and have a blast.

*I like long walks, especially when they are taken by people who annoy me.*

—Noel Coward

# Chapter Six
# The Go-Go Goddess

Parties, bars, and hanging out are just a piece of a comprehensive diva plan of recovery. To become a superstar, you have to work toward excelling in your career and building outside interests that are satisfying and meaningful.

## Job Junkie

Your job is a big part of your life, so you might as well make the most of it. Right after a breakup, you probably had trouble focusing on the tasks at hand. But now that you're feeling better, it's time to put some energy back into your career and work your way up the ladder to Chief Executive Diva. Climbing to the top takes motivation, talent, and a little bit of luck, but using your ex as inspiration, you can do anything. Just focus on the image of him sending his resume to you in search of a job. It will get a fire burning inside of you, one that will incinerate his resume and anything else he sends along with it.

A breakup can be an excellent wake-up call, forcing you to re-examine every part of your life. You might realize you don't

*Women now have choices. They can be married, not married, have a job, not have a job, be married with children, unmarried with children. Men have the same choice they've always had: work or prison.*

*—Paraphrased quote by Tim Allen*

like your job or you aren't making the progress you want to make. Perhaps you've been putting off work and investing most of your energy into the relationship. Regardless of where you are right now with your career, you can develop a plan that will get you where you want to be tomorrow. Traveling the long road to Chief Executive Diva is easier for sassy women who find the shortcuts. If you know you put off your own job search because you were waiting to see what would happen with the relationship, make up for lost time now. Get to work immediately making a list of the steps you'll take to make things happen. As you devise your own plan for getting ahead, assess your level of satisfaction with the actual work you're doing. It might seem easy in comparison to the twenty-four-hour-a-day baby-sitting job you felt like you were doing when you dated your ex, but try to look at it objectively. If you do not feel any sense of reward or satisfaction from your work, get out now and look for a more fulfilling job.

Try to remind yourself of the top ways to land a new gig. Sending your resume blindly to headhunters and job postings is not the most efficient way to go about business. Try some of the following strategies for landing the job of your dreams.

### Talk to People You Know

The best way to get your resume in someone's hands, and to get it looked at, is to send it through a personal contact, along with a great big basket of fruit.

### Showcase Relevant Talents

A resume is not supposed to be a catchall cataloging every one of your skills, classes, jobs, and talents. Though many employers will find it fascinating that you floored your ex in two seconds flat with your mountain bike, it might not be a skill relevant to the job at hand.

### Don't Limit Yourself

Don't let the qualifications section of a job description deter you from applying. Many jobs are malleable and can be fashioned to fit the person who is hired. Send your resume if you want the job, as long as you think you have the necessary skills. You can always spin the technical expertise you acquired from carrying out your sassy battle plan into bullet points that far outshine any degree.

### Go on Every Interview

Sometimes even if the job you're interviewing for isn't right for you, the person conducting the interview will take you

*I always wanted to be somebody, but I should have been more specific.*

*—Lily Tomlin*

upstairs and introduce you to someone else in the company who is hiring. Go even if it's just for the practice. Also, never rule out a prospective job just because the headhunter made it sound crappy. Their powers of description are never their strength. You can learn a thing or two about stalking from them, though.

### Always Take a Step Up

If you are changing jobs in the same city and field, negotiate a larger salary increase and ask for more vacation than they are offering. If you are changing fields or cities, pay close attention to what you should be getting for your skills, and don't sell yourself short.

**Diva Boss**

When your ex finally starts working for you because he can't find a job anywhere else, use these phrases regularly to make work more fun:

- Fetch me coffee, boy.
- There's an error in this 300-page report you did, but I'm not going to tell you where it is. Let's see if you can find it on your own.
- Why is this heading off center? You need to stop making these glaring errors in aesthetics.
- I can't give you your year-end bonus because of all those times you took thirty-five minutes for lunch instead of thirty. We really needed you here, and you let us down.
- We're going to have to ask you to share your office with Wendy, the new manager we hired. Wendy is the lesbian women's rights activist referred to us through the Manhaters of America Organization. I'm sure you two will get along splendidly.

*I've no time for broads who want to rule the world alone. Without men, who'd do up the zipper on the back of your dress?*

—Bette Davis

## Rely On Yourself

Keep in mind that those who do not find any satisfaction in their work rely entirely on their significant other for fulfillment. This situation is a dangerous one to be in, given that no man will ever be able to fulfill 100 percent of any woman's needs. Your partner should be an asset to your already fabulous life, not the beam that keeps the entire structure from toppling over.

## Enjoy Your Work

The more you enjoy your work, the more money you will make doing it. You can use your extra cash to spiff up your wardrobe, invest in the markets, or buy the company your ex works for so you can fire him on the spot.

A diva on the road to stardom takes control of her career and makes the decisions necessary to get to a place where she's happy. Now might be a good time to reassess your level of satisfaction with your work and make a change for the better.

*I don't know much about being a millionaire, but I'll bet I'd be darling at it.*

—Dorothy Parker

## Diva Do More

Your action plan is not over at the end of the workday. In fact, it's just beginning. Most of your new pursuits will be in the off hours as you fill the time your ex once occupied with new, exciting activities and interests. If you remain as busy as possible, you'll feel fulfilled and will have less time to think about him and the breakup. The more you're out, the more people you will come in contact with and the better chance you'll have of meeting a great new guy. You also might learn a new skill or talent you can use in the future to make your life better, or your ex's life worse.

The standard post-breakup time fillers—pottery class, museums, walks through the park—are a good place to start, but you'll find more motivation to stay busy if you think about activities that fulfill the following criteria.

### Things He Thought You Didn't Do Well

If he made fun of your cooking, become an expert chef. If he thought you were bad in bed, start your own escort business, name it after him, and host his coworkers.

### Things He Never Wanted to Do with You

If you love wine-tasting events and he always refused to accompany you, go alone or with a girlfriend, and keep an eye out

*Men are like a job; they pay for dinner and they can be rewarding but more often than not, they are a big pain in the ass.*
*—Anonymous*

**Sporty Diva**
Feeling athletic beyond your workout regimen? Join a softball team or try your hand at tennis. Never be a poor loser. Save that role for your ex, because he's a natural.

for worthy men who like to sample wines too. The equation "wine + men = great post-breakup night out" is one worth committing to memory.

### Things He Made Fun of All the Time

If he thought racquetball was lame, now you have all the more reason to try it.

Just as tears can motivate you during the grieving stage, his lack of enthusiasm for your interests can motivate you to try new things and take part in the activities that are important to you. There's great satisfaction in becoming the antithesis of his ideal woman by doing everything he hated.

Remember, though, that reaching your full fabulous diva potential means doing things just because you want to do them, not because they're influenced by your ex—or by anyone else, for that matter. Dust off some of the dreams you set aside when you met the former Mr. Wonderful.

### Educational Pursuits

If you've always thought about getting an MBA or going back to school to make a career change, maybe now is the time to do it. Classes and homework hanging over your head will definitely keep you occupied, so you won't have time to think about him.

Sassy Scoop

Post his phone number on the campus bulletin board as "pizza delivery."

Top Diva Electives

- Ancient Torture Techniques . . . to be used on an ex when needed.
- How Criminals Escape the Law . . . to escape suspicion and create a good alibi.
- Foreign Language . . . to curse in front of him without his knowledge.
- Corporate Finance . . . to calculate the return on the investment you've made in your ex.

    TIP: If you can't fit the Corporate Finance elective into your schedule, you can still figure out the return on your investment in the relationship using these easy steps:

1. Put a monetary value on everything you gave him—time, food, gifts, travel, and anything else important.
2. Add it all up. Did you get back what you gave to him?
3. If the answer is "no," submit a bill to him for reimbursement, making sure to tag on a healthy interest rate.

If taking a class doesn't appeal to you, why not read about a useful topic at home? Find a medical library and explore textbooks on "performing a vasectomy operation." Read motivational books about people who have overcome crisis and done something wonderful with their lives. Or, just frequent the bookstore so that when a hot guy walks your way, you can ask him to help you find the book titled *Delicious Bookstore Babe.* If it doesn't exist, start writing.

### Artistic Pursuits

If you feel more artsy than you do bookish, lots of options lie before you. All it takes is some super glue and a little imagination.

Create a time capsule using an old coffee can. Put in picture of your ex, on which you've written "Spawn of the Devil." Bury it deep within the ground. If you're lucky, when a new civilization digs it up thousands of years from now, he will be categorized appropriately in their first encyclopedia. *Sassy Scoop*

### Try Jewelry Making

Make yourself a gorgeous necklace to wear out at night. When you run into your ex, tell him it was a gift your new boyfriend bought you in Paris.

### Become a Seamstress Extraordinaire

If you're handy with a sewing machine, pick up fabric and make a sexy one-of-a-kind skirt for the next party you attend. You'll feel great because you created it yourself, and it will be a wonderful conversation starter when new guys come up to talk to you. If you don't know how to sew, this is a great time to learn, before you get too busy fending off the diva worshipers.

### Take Artsy Classes

Now is also a great time to take acting classes and get involved in theater or film. You'll find theatrical training useful when you're trying to act calm and confident in front of him or his friends. This training will also help you if you run into his new girlfriend and you have to act like she's not a homely tramp, but a nice person with good taste in men.

**Diva Español**
Practice your Spanish when you run into your ex. Hint: *pendejo* means jackass.

### Find Your Inner Picasso

Paint "you suck" in colorful letters across his car, his front window, and his lawn. Then, paint a mural of him naked in his courtyard. Be creative.

Remember that you may be able to profit from whatever interest you cultivate and hone. Turn your love of jewelry into a line of pieces for sale on consignment. Sell crafts or other creations over the Internet. Find a way to spend your free time, disparage your ex, and make money off the entire operation. Then thank him for his inspiration on the last page of your memoirs.

**Sassy Scoop**
If you like to draw, sketch a large picture of him. At your next girls'-night-in party, everyone can take turns playing "Pin the dart on the jackass."

### *Cooking for One*

Enjoy cooking and entertaining? Try some of these recipes for the busy diva hostess:

- **Appetizer:** Cut up cheese and crackers. Lay out on plate.
- **Chicken:** Call local caterer. Order chicken entrée. Be sure to specify delivery time.

- **Soup:** Open can, pour into pan, and heat on low. Serve in a bowl or mug.
- **Breakfast:** Open box, pour cereal into bowl, cover with milk, and serve.
- **Italian meal:** Call pizza delivery phone number twenty minutes before guests arrive.
- **Chocolate chip cookies:** Buy chocolate chip cookie dough in freezer section of store; slice and bake.
- **Chocolate milkshake:** Put milk and chocolate ice cream in blender. Blend.

## *Noble Pursuits*

If you enjoy volunteering, get involved in a local organization that needs a helping hand. While you're at it, sign your ex's name on every volunteer list citywide, and encourage them to call him regularly. Volunteering can be a great way to meet new people, stay active and make yourself feel better by helping people who are worse off than you are.

### Rebuild Low-Income Housing

Learn to hammer, drill, paint, and caulk all while building units for the needy. With your new skills, put a nice layer of bright gold paint on your ex's house and caulk his front door around the edges so it won't budge.

### Volunteer with Youth

Plan and supervise activities for neighborhood kids in need. It's a great way to have a positive impact on the youth in your community and a negative impact on your ex. Orchestrate a big game of kickball near his house. Tell the kids you have candy ready and waiting for whomever first breaks a window with the ball.

### Assist the Elderly

Through local programs you can take senior citizens shopping, help them clean the house, and plan visits just to keep them from getting lonely. If your ex has elderly people in his family, try to find a way to help them, too. If you hang in there long enough you might be able to pilfer his inheritance legally.

### Get Political

Attend women's rights rallies or seminars. These events by their very nature make women feel unified and give them a shared sense of purpose. You'll have the opportunity to network and learn something about the latest issues these groups are tackling. You'll also have a chance to meet new fellow divas with edge whom you can integrate into your glam posse.

Whatever your interests are, you can find a program or organization to indulge them. So fill up your free time with all the activities you can, keep busy, and continue to build your new life as a superstar.

## Traveling for Work or Pleasure

Sometimes, staying in an area ridden with relationship reminders is just not a good idea. If you can't get him out of your head and you still feel ill every time you drive by the street where he lives, therapeutic travel might be just the thing for you. Traveling doesn't have to be costly, and you don't need to go far to gain the perspective you need. Of course, if you can afford to re-enter the scene in a faraway tropical paradise, by all means go. However, if a day trip is all you have time or money for, you can still glean great benefits.

However long your trip, a new, unexplored destination will open up your mind and give you some distance from your problems and the people in your life. It will also provide you with a host of vengeful tactics you can't use from home.

- Head for a historical battleground from the Revolutionary or Civil wars. Send him postcards featuring active battle scenes and write "wish you had been there."
- Etch his number in bathrooms at rest stops. Ensure that he gets calls from around the globe.
- Send him disparaging mail with a faraway postmark.
- Distribute regular updates of your encounters with cute foreign men to everyone on your e-mail list. "Accidentally" include him.
- Bring back a special souvenir for him—a foreign concoction guaranteed to cause Montezuma's revenge.
- Discover annoying tourist traps and recommend them to him upon your return.

The bottom line is—just go-go-go. The busier you are, the more people you'll meet and the more fulfilled you'll feel. The key to having a great relationship with anyone is having a fantastic life as an independent person. If you have your own interests and pursuits that excite you, you'll be a more interesting, fun-loving and happy person. Other people will sense that. Those with no fulfillment in their own life, like your ex, will be annoyed by your success, but confident, energetic people will be attracted to you. You'll send out positive vibes and those vibes will come back to you in the form of fun, friends, and even more social opportunities.

## A Major Life Makeover

Sometimes a vacation and even a change of lifestyle are not enough to give you the perspective you need after a breakup. If you still can't ditch thoughts of him and move on with ease, you might be a good candidate for a major life makeover—a move to a new city or country. To reap the many benefits of a big move, a diva must first get past the initial fear of change. If you've never left your hometown or you are a sucker for routine, a major life makeover will be more difficult for you, but it might be more necessary, too.

Making a big move on your own can help you build confidence in yourself and forget about the things in your past that make you unhappy. It might be the refreshing start you need right after a big breakup. Because you are a sassy single, you have the luxury of freedom. You are free to go where you want to go and explore new horizons with nothing to hold you back. You can move to a new city, start again with a clean slate, and leave all your troubles behind you.

### *Benefits of a Major Life Makeover*

- Nothing in your new city will remind you of him.
- You'll have a good reason to buy the new designer luggage you've been eyeing.
- You will meet people who don't even know he exists.
- You will have access to activities you've never tried before.
- No one will be around to judge you based on your past.
- Your sense of inner stability will be stronger because you will realize that even when the world around you changes, who you are does not.
- You'll get the chance to furnish a different place with funky new housewares.
- You'll get to meet all the cute on-site customer service men when they come to hook up your cable.
- You will feel more confident once you learn firsthand that you have what it takes to survive in an unfamiliar place.

- If you move to a big city, you'll have a greater number of new single diva friends at your disposal.
- If you move to a smaller town, you'll enjoy the calm, relaxing atmosphere and lower cost of living.

Putting yourself into new, challenging situations is a great way to build your self-confidence and widen your perspective of life. When you move after a breakup, you will recover faster and be happier again in record time because you won't have to face memories of him at every turn. So if you are unhappy with your life the way it is, research a major life makeover, get a friend onboard to go with you if that's the only way you think you can do it, and then get to work on making the big change happen. This move is one that requires the utmost sass, but it will send you flying down the road to divadom at unparalleled speeds.

*Rub in Your Success*

Rub in your success . . . or do you really need to? The best way to get on his nerves is to look like you've moved on. And if you've been busy making friends, being social, and getting involved in new activities, chances are you really *have* begun to move on.

**Go for the Bull's-Eye**

You wouldn't aim blindly into a crowd hoping to hit your ex. You would take a step back, aim, and then fire. Apply the same process to your personal life. Don't try to do too much at once. Zero in on one target, then hit it hard and fast.

Learning to place yourself as top priority is critical to your recovery and to your happiness. Never give your all to a guy with the expectation that it will strengthen your relationship with him. A strong relationship consists of two people who know how to be happy on their own and simply enhance each other's lives when they are together. So whether you plan to get involved with another guy someday or you simply want to get over this one and live the solo life for a while, get to work on making yourself happy and fulfilled with friends, fun, and activities galore.

Make time to do whatever you deem important regardless of who you're dating, how difficult your job is, and what your circumstances are in life. You are independently fabulous, and you deserve to be happy on your own. A guy should only add to your already fulfilling life. He should never *be* your life.

# Chapter Seven
# Celebrate the Single Life

Now that you're feeling good and you're back on the social scene, you will begin to forget you even have an ex. He'll still pop into your head occasionally, no doubt. You'll think of him when you hear a song on the radio or see that Hooters billboard he loves along the highway. But these thoughts will be fleeting and won't make you quite as sad as they once did.

Nevertheless, at times little doubts will creep into your head and bring back your breakup blues. The wedding announcement that "could have been you and him," or your Aunt's poignant question about your love life, can send you back into a downward spiral if they hit at the wrong time. This section will help you ward off these pests and celebrate your single life in style.

You might notice while you're out that you are particularly aware of being single. It will seem like couples are everywhere. You'll see smiling girls wearing engagement rings, cute guys

**Not Necessary, But Nice to Have**
We don't have to go so far as to say "a woman needs a man like a fish needs a bicycle," but we can strive for "a woman needs a man like a cute summer dress needs just the right sandals." The right sandals are not essential, but they really do add a touch of style to your ensemble.

kissing their girlfriends on the cheek, and birds flying in twos overhead.

Don't panic—this stage of the recovery process won't last long. Cheerful people in love are not stalking you. As hard as it is to have perspective during this time, keep telling yourself that this phase will pass, some of the people you see will break up, and someday you'll be the one with your life together, comforting them.

Sometimes breaking up is even more difficult because of the messages that bombard you in your day-to-day life. "Diamonds are forever." "Discounted vacations for two." It can seem like everywhere you turn your family, friends, and the media are trying to marry you off. These messages don't have to get you down and set you back a step in the recovery process. You can handle them with sass and learn to appreciate being single for all it has to offer.

## The Perks of Singlehood

There are many benefits of being single that a diva might not appreciate until they are gone. Take time to celebrate these perks now so you'll never look back at your single years and wish you had spent them differently. As a fabulous single you can:

* Spend your free time any way you wish and never be interrupted by the roar of a stadium crowd coming from the TV room.

* Eat an entire carton of ice cream in one sitting . . . guilt-free, with no interruptions.

* Pursue whatever dream you have, even if it's to fill up an entire room with chic handbags from every major city in the world.

* Get excited for a night on the town knowing you'll have a blast with outrageous single friends.

* Rack up big credit card and cell phone bills without being subject to review by the spending warden.

* Flirt and date with lots of guys just for the heck of it, and find a new boy toy to kiss just for fun.

* Take a solo trip at a moment's notice with friends or any cute guy in need.

* Use the bathroom whenever you want without dodging a hurricane of dirt, hair, and other disgusting unidentified particles.

* Live "in-law free."

Valuing your single life is hardest after a breakup, but rest assured, right when you're about to tie the knot, you'll wish you could go back for a while and relive your fun-filled days of solo bliss. You have the opportunity to appreciate them now, so keep the perks of singlehood at the fore of your mind. Celebrate all the wonderful things that make this time so magical.

*Why did God create men? Because vibrators can't mow the lawn.*

—Madonna

## A Single Moment

"Moments" aren't just for old people anymore. They have senior moments; you will have a single moment or two. A single moment happens when a situation makes you so uncomfortable about being single that you wish a monster would rear its ugly head and bite off your ringless finger. The best way to tackle a single moment is to recognize it for what it is and then to counter it by reminding yourself of all the perks of singlehood. Here are some common "single moments":

* You grab lunch at a diner by yourself and you think the people nearby feel sorry for you because you're alone.
* Your cousin five years your junior shows up with her new fiancé at your family's holiday dinner and everyone turns to ask you when you're planning to follow suit.
* You're filling out forms and you have to write down your maiden name and your last name. You only have a maiden name, and you hate it.
* You try to buy take-out for one and the restaurant won't deliver it because the order isn't large enough.
* People turn to you at a party when they start talking about

**Don't Be a Wedding Wannabe**
If someone's engagement or wedding announcement makes you feel like you're behind the pack, take a picture of your face and put it over the bride's. Would you want to be married to that guy? Chances are the suggestion alone is enough to send you running.

single women, and ask you for your opinion as if you are an authority on the subject.

✳ You find out that one of your exes—the one that was the biggest playboy on the planet—is getting married.

✳ You're waiting for your friend at a bar and she's fifteen minutes late. You are sure everyone around you thinks you are being stood up by a guy.

If you have a single moment, combat it by making a quick mental laundry list of all the reasons why being single is fabulous. If that doesn't work, call up your married friend and let her tell you how she chased her husband with a butter knife last week and laced his omelet with hot pepper so he'd stop talking during breakfast. Most important, remember that your thoughts are not imprinted on your forehead for the world to see. People don't have to know when you're having a moment of insecurity. Just do some positive self-talk (not out loud, or people will think you're crazy) and find your way back to divadom.

## The Single Police

Even if you are happiest flying solo, there are people out there who have the ability to change all that with a simple question or insinuation. They are called the single police. The single police include your mother, who lays on the "I'll never get to see my grandchildren" guilt routine, all those relatives who quiz you about your love life over the holidays, and the Madison Avenue executives who make the 1950s-style "mom doing laundry" commercials. When you're single, it can seem as if there is a huge conspiracy among the wedded masses to bring you over to their side.

Fortunately, things are changing, and independent female role models are popping up here and there in the media. But they alone are not enough to stave off the single police. To really give single girls everywhere the freedom to celebrate their singlehood, each diva must take it upon herself to confront the single police with sass. Familiarize yourself with the members of the force so you'll be prepared to muster saucy comebacks and put them in their place.

The list of single police in your life may be long and varied or short and annoying, but either way they share one purpose: to question you about your love life at inopportune times and to preach to you the merits of settling down sooner rather than later.

### Officer Mom

*Stats:* She longs for grandchildren. She worries you aren't moving fast enough. She has a faint twinge of jealousy when she sees your youthful face and realizes you have the chance to meet someone better than your lobotomized father. Every time you're in a fight with a boyfriend she lectures, "Maybe you should go easier on that guy." That "mom knows best" tone hits your inner soul like a ruthless dagger filled with poisonous chicken noodle soup.

But beware of the other side of the coin—even an ultrasupportive mom can freak out when you least expect it. All of a sudden she tosses out a shifty comment like, "Did you see Michelle's wedding announcement? An autumn wedding . . . sigh." Your mother has turned into the passive-aggressive wedding hawk. It is ten times worse if you are the eldest or only child, and a hundred times worse if you are going through a breakup.

*Motives:* Mom joined the force with good intentions. You

are her daughter, and she only wants what's best for you (plus a few grandchildren for herself). She thought by joining the single police she could inspire you to get moving and find her a son-in-law.

### Officer Extended Family Member(s)

*Stats:* These folks are the foot soldiers of the single police, and you'll suffer their interrogations mostly around the holidays. These aunts, uncles, and cousins have nothing to say to you, so they try their hand at useless small talk. What other questions do they have for their young niece than "Oh honey, so have you met that special guy yet?" You want to respond, "Yes, actually, but he's dead now and you will be too if you don't leave me alone."

The same conversations may occur when you're in the presence of other random acquaintances like work people, your hairdresser, or your mailman. They ask that famed question, "When are you getting married?" and you shrug and fumble over an explanation or try to change the subject. It is next to impossible to blurt out, "I'm not dating anyone," without launching into your rehearsed string of explanations.

*Motives:* Don't think for one minute that they are trying to annoy you intentionally. For them, it is mindless and effortless. These people joined the single police by accident. They are

*Old ladies used to come up to me at weddings, pinch my arm and say, "You're next." They stopped when I started doing the same thing to them at funerals.*

—Unknown

unable to come up with an original topic for small talk, so they resort to the tried-and-true topics: dating, marriage, and babies. It's part of the status quo, and it just so happens to be a part we loathe after a breakup.

### Officer Advertising Executive

*Stats:* This officer creates commercials full of happy couples giving each other diamond jewelry against a snowy backdrop. Even if you flip the channel when these savvy productions come on, little pieces of them stick in your head and remind you that Officer Ad Executive thinks you need to get married. Remind yourself of the real couples you know—the ones who actually get cold in the snow and argue about who is going to put salt on the icy steps—and you'll undermine Officer Ad Exec's fictional world.

*Motives:* This officer has one goal, which is to sell products to consumers everywhere. This inspired him to flash his badge your way.

### Officer Old Person

*Stats:* Officers are the most innocent members of the single police. They are, well, old. They lived during a different time,

**What Really Gave You Comfort?**
Try to separate the pressures you feel about being single from your breakup angst. It's important to figure out whether what you really miss is your ex or just the shield he provided from the single police.

**Widow Wisdom**

If an old woman asks you when you are getting married, reply with, "Are you sure I should really consider spending the rest of my life with one guy?" She'll laugh, wink, and know exactly what you mean. There is a reason why women outlive their husbands.

when all women knew how to cook and men knew how to do household handy work. Their world was different. They think men still work in the coal mines and order brides from overseas. They have no idea how much the world has changed, and that now you can order a groom over the Internet if you wish.

*Motives:* These officers stumble onto the force in the dark. They are genuine and innocent. They would resign tomorrow if they thought their questions were bothering you. Remember how different their world was, and appreciate how far singlekind has come since they were your age.

### *Officer Homemaker*

*Stats:* She's your married friend or coworker, sucked into a swirling vortex of domestic bliss. You love her to death, but you often wonder if she inherited a recessive gene that made her fall out of touch with the trials of domestic divadom. Where you see a crying, slobbering child, she sees an adorable little cherub in need. Where you see a large plot of dirt, she sees an opportunity to use her new gardening set.

*Motives:* Officer Homemaker wants you to share her daily joy. She's eager for you to fall in love and then come over and cook a roast with her.

## *Fighting the Single Police with Sassy Comebacks*

After a breakup, it can seem like everywhere you turn, someone is there asking you annoying questions about your personal life. But as a confident diva, you can handle any questions that come your way. Just let your sassy side inspire fun, outrageous comebacks.

**Question:** Why is a pretty girl like you still single?
**Response:** Why is an ugly person like you still married?

Get the single police off your back with the all-time favorite response to nosy people everywhere: "I'm a lesbian until further notice."

**Sassy Scoop**

**Question:** When are you getting married?
**Response:** After seeing your husband, I've decided it's just not worth it.

**Question:** Aren't you tired of the singles scene?
**Response:** Actually, I'm not single. I'm living in sin and loving every minute of it.

**Question:** Aren't you worried about your biological clock?
**Response:** I'm not having any kids because I'm afraid they'll inherit some of your traits. (For use with extended family only.)

**Question:** What are you doing for Valentine's Day?
**Response:** That's the day of my big OB/GYN appointment. Can you believe the doctor said . . .

**Question:** Don't you hate living alone?
**Response:** It's not living alone that bugs me. It's my mummified ex-boyfriend in the corner that really drives me nuts.

**V-Day Fun**

Tackle Valentine's Day head-on. Never hide from the monster. Rally your single friends and organize the biggest party of your life at a place that's rowdy with tacky décor, great margaritas, loud Mexican music, and piñatas hanging overhead. When the owner hands you a stick, swing away with all your might at the candy-filled jackass.

Try to keep in mind that people often ask these types of questions when they don't have anything else to say. They aren't necessarily making a conscious effort to bug you (believe it or not). Though this knowledge doesn't make them any less annoying, it will help you take their inquiries less personally and keep your spunky spirit intact.

*Myths about the Single Life*

Myths about the single life have evolved over generations and are perpetuated today by people who are out of touch with the sassy side of singlehood. Even those with benign intentions might pass these stereotypes along and keep your single celebration at bay. Familiarize yourself with these myths so you can eliminate them along with the badges of the single police.

A single woman:

- Can't be complete without a guy in her life
- Turns twenty-six or twenty-eight or thirty or whatever age, freaks out, and wants to elope
- Hates holidays
- Is a bitter Cruella De Vil (but has cats instead of polka-dot puppies)

*How wrong it is for a woman to expect the man to build the world she wants, rather than to create it herself.*

—Anais Nin

- Has a disease
- Cares far too much about her career
- Is only single because she hasn't met a man
- Is a butch lesbian gym teacher

None of these myths are true, yet enough people buy into the list to keep it going. For fun, rewrite each myth and add the phrase, "but she enjoys beating her ex"—something like this: A single woman hates holidays, but she enjoys beating her ex. A single woman is a butch lesbian gym teacher, but she enjoys beating her ex. Try tagging on that phrase to any unpalatable remark you receive. It makes life much more entertaining. Exercises like these help you release your frustrations and they also add an element of truth to otherwise preposterous stereotypes.

## Treasure Your Space

You can learn to celebrate being single by building the space around you into your own personal paradise. Your space is not just your house or apartment, but any part of your world you claim as your own. It's your style, your favorite spots in town, your values, the music you love, or your idea of a great dinner. It encompasses all things that reflect your own individuality.

Right after the breakup, it is important to identify those parts of your world that reflect you and separate them from those things you've embraced simply because they were part of your ex's life. You probably have at least one CD or article of clothing you bought solely because he liked it. Perhaps you've left your bedroom the same because you remember the way he used to lay on the bed, stick his foot up in the air, and turn off the light switch with his toe. Celebrate your own life as a single diva by erasing these marks left by your ex and replacing them with things that represent you.

### *Your Living Space, a.k.a. the Bachelorette Pad*

The most obvious place to start your space renovation is your house or apartment, the beloved B-pad. Rearrange it in a different way, switch the wall hangings, buy yourself a new appliance or electronic gadget, and get a couple of extra lamps. Turn the B-pad into a new world with no reminders of your ex. Don't forget to sterilize anything he's touched. You don't want his germs on your hands, or his lingering smell in your nose. Get new sheets so the new guy you are about to meet has a nice, clean place to sleep. You want the B-pad to be a world unsullied by your ex's presence (but filled with his presents, like that cute little necklace you never gave back).

Next, make a list of all the things you want to purchase and all the things you want to otherwise change about the place where you live. Then just do it. Some women think that if they buy their

**Shed Some Light**
New lights will change the mood of the B-pad. While you're out buying them, see if you can get your hands on a flashing floodlight to install outside your ex's bedroom window.

own residence or seriously invest in home furnishings or electronics, they are sending a message to the "dating gods" that they do not want a significant other. You are the dating god-

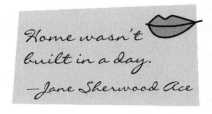

*Home wasn't built in a day.*
—Jane Sherwood Ace

dess, so you trump the dating gods. If you die in a freak accident, your final memories should involve a queen-sized bed, a plush living-room set, and a cappuccino maker, not an empty "I'm waiting until I'm married" apartment full of secondhand goods. Don't wait to buy the things you really want for the B-pad.

### Public Personal Space

Identify your public personal space, the places that feel like they are your own. Maybe you spend time in the park, a coffee shop, the bookstore, or a favorite sunbathing place. Or maybe you favor a nice bench with a view of the men's lacrosse fields. Anywhere can be your public personal space. It is simply the place you go because you selected it and you enjoy it.

It is easy to get caught up in day-to-day life and forget to take time out to think and relax. But once you feel connected to a public personal space, you will enjoy going there and will do it more often. Learning to have fun on your own is an important skill in life. Once you can enjoy being by yourself, you are well on your way to being an independent diva. "Loneliness" will never again be a factor in any dating equation.

**Treat Yourself**
Take yourself out on the town to eat, shop, or see a movie. You don't need a guy to go on a date.

*If your success is not on your own terms, if it looks good to the world but does not feel good in your heart, it is not success at all.*

*—Anna Quindlen*

### Your "You" Space

Your "you" space encompasses all the things about you that make you a unique person in the world—your values, your beliefs, your style and experiences. No diva is complete without chiseling herself into a prime reflection of who she is and what she stands for. You've already worked on building up your self-confidence. Now add pride in who you are and a willingness to stand up for what you believe in. Whether you are fun, creative, conservative, or caring, be proud of those qualities that uniquely define you, and use them to contribute in your own way to the world.

Likewise, ditch those parts of your style that are based on the preferences of your ex, your friends, or media trends, and become the ultimate sophistabitch. A sophistabitch is a woman who emanates confidence all the time, whose attitude, values, and appearance say "I am the person I feel comfortable being and not what someone else wants me to be." A guy can easily transform a diva into the cover model for *Fashion Faux Pas* magazine if she lets him. Most men don't realize that a bright orange string bikini and inline skates are not in vogue for a Friday night out. And if he can mess up your wardrobe, imagine what he can do to your attitude and beliefs if they aren't firmly grounded. Become the ultimate sophistabitch and you'll never feel the need to change in order to fit someone else's image of what you should be. The right people will appreciate you for who you are.

You'll know you are a sophistabitch when:

* Your incredibly popular friend recommends you wear leg warmers to her next party. You show up in your favorite outfit, minus the warmers, with no fear of her fashion wrath.
* Everyone you know has the same cute little clutch, but you can't deal with strapless bags. You dare to be different with your own mini-messenger, or you purchase the clutch and sew on a sparkling shoulder strap.
* The old fabric shower curtain is just too cool to throw out. You embrace the fabric like it's imported silk and make adorable pillows for your couch.
* Someone asks you what you think about the latest gubernatorial candidate. At first you just hear goober and think of your ex. But then you state your opinion with sass, unfazed by the slew of criticisms that follow.
* You decide you want to start your own business, but your friend tells you it is impossible. You go for it anyway. Years later, you buy out her company and make her sit in a basement cubicle.

### The Sophistabitch Within
Remember that other women are not sailing through life on a yacht filled with hot men and martinis while you're sitting on shore alone drinking stale beer. You have what they do. Never feel intimidated. Just step up your attitude, and you will become what you believe you are.

When you treasure your space, you build your world into a place that reflects your style, preferences, and values. You fully celebrate your life as an independent goddess.

Always be a sassy diva without reservations, unless they're at a chic restaurant.

When you do get involved with a man, you have boundaries in place. You know what tastes and values you can't and won't surrender, because they are a fundamental part of you. Your self-assurance eliminates from your dating pool those men who feel threatened by your independent side and those who don't appreciate it. If your self-assurance alone doesn't get rid of them, pull out your stylish wooden club and wield it wildly.

## Trust in the Universe

Part of celebrating your single life is trusting that the universe has something in store for you and that you are exactly where you are supposed to be at this time. Maybe you have certain lessons you need to learn right now and they will make your relationships better in the future. Maybe you are supposed to cultivate a certain talent or take advantage of career opportunities, and a guy would only prevent you from doing so. Perhaps it is your divinely appointed task to torment your ex for the rest of his adult life (a task you can fulfill quickly by shortening the span a bit). As you move forward toward stardom, gain even greater perspective in your life by doing these three hokey things.

### *Try to Imagine Yourself at Age Ninety*

Knowing you only have a few years left, is there anything you wish you had done? Are there things you worried about or

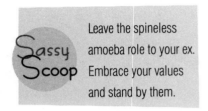

Leave the spineless amoeba role to your ex. Embrace your values and stand by them.

felt sad about that you wish you hadn't wasted your time on? How will you spend your remaining days? Playing bingo? Getting your cataracts corrected? Or doing something else? Begin living your life today with the intensity you would feel if you knew you only had a short time left.

## "What Goes Around Comes Around"

Test this principle out by doing something each day that helps another person or contributes something good to the world. Hold the door for an annoying person. Be patient with the grumpy cashier. Make it a habit to do something positive that is completely beyond what you would normally do. You will get back what you put into life (and thankfully, so will your bastard ex).

## Think Back to Where You Were Five Years Ago

Do you still have the same problems, concerns, and priorities you had then? Your life as you know it today will change as well. Even though it might seem like time is standing still, you will wake up one morning and realize you have completely moved on.

You might never understand entirely how your current situation fits into your life plan. In fact, you might feel certain that

*Change is inevitable—except from a vending machine.*

*—Robert G. Gallagher*

some long-gone relative who hates you is messing with your head from above. But a diva celebrating the single life is optimistic and believes that all her experiences will leave her better off in some way. Use this time to learn to love your independence and to appreciate your world without another person in it. Then when someone special does come along, he'll be a great enhancement to your superstar life.

## Chapter Eight
# Déjà Vu

A year goes by, you're feeling better, your life is back in order, and maybe you've even moved to a new city. You haven't exchanged obligatory e-mails or phone calls with him in several months. You've finally arrived at a place in your life where you are happy without him. You're dating new guys, and even though you think of him on occasion, you by no means get sick over him like you used to.

Then one day you are window-shopping on your way to the post office, just strolling along, enjoying the afternoon and taking in the sights. Out of nowhere, you hear the ugly screeches of a nearby man-monster. When you look up, you cringe in fear and loathing. There he is, across the street, and he's looking your way. You dodge wildly past people in your path, running for your life, but to no avail—he hunts you down and grabs your arm. You are certain he's about to chew up your ego, spit it out like it's an old piece of bubblegum, and continue on his way. But instead, he starts talking your ear off, and you're caught dealing with him once again. You didn't even realize he was living nearby. Where did he come from, and who has been cutting his hair? Is he smiling, or is something wrong with his face? You are about to begin what will be a month of telltale déjà vu.

## Rerun Risk

Even the most horrific relationships sometimes begin again, long after you thought they ended. A rerun relationship can either be the greatest thing in your life or a grave error that sends you back to square one in your recovery. Though you might be thinking that you'd never entertain the idea of a rerun relationship with your ex, keep this section on hand just in case. It will help you make a wise decision on how to proceed if a rerun ever happens to you.

Some divas are more at risk for having a rerun relationship than others. To tell if you are a rerun risk, answer the following questions:

**Do you still think there is a possibility that you will end up with your ex for the long haul?**

If, a year after the breakup, you are still holding on to the idea of him as a possible long-term beau, you are a major rerun risk. To get over a guy you have to let go of him completely. Holding on to the hope that it will pan out one day does nothing more than mess up your chances of becoming an independently happy diva. It also really lowers the odds that you will have a meaningful relationship with someone else. Though there's always a chance that you will see your ex years from now and a spark will ignite, the only spark you have any control over right now is the one you light to burn his pictures and letters. Anything that happens in the future will happen on its own. Therefore you must live your life as if you'll never get back together with him instead of banking on the dream of a relationship that you don't have the power to bring about.

### Do you compare every guy you meet to him?

Are you stuck in the mode of thinking he is the greatest guy who ever walked? If so, have someone pinch you immediately with a powerful device, like the Jaws of Life. A guy who breaks up with you cannot possibly be that great—he couldn't even see the diva before his very eyes. If you still have him on a pedestal, you are a big rerun risk. Refer back to "Dealing Like a Diva" (Chapter 1), and pull the jackass down hard and fast.

## Quiz  Are You Really over Your Ex?

Are you still in love with your ex a year later? To find out, take this quiz.

1. Someone tells you he took his new girlfriend on a romantic trip to the world's largest beer brewery, followed by dinner at Hooters. You think:

    a. Knowing him and his obvious lack of taste in women—if he knew a good woman when he saw one, he wouldn't have broken up with me—the new girl is probably thrilled with his plan.
    b. What a cheap, selfish, classless bastard. He hasn't changed.
    c. Wow. He has such a great sense of humor. It's so fantastic how he blends history, culture, and fine cuisine.

    *If you picked "c," you are still suffering from poor vision. You see goodness where there clearly is none, a strong indication that you are not over him.*

2. You find out he finally passed the bar after taking it for the fifth time. You think:
   a. Congratulations to Mr. Clueless. Imagine if I'd married him. I would have had to spend the rest of my life worrying every day that he was going to be fired from his job for idiocy.
   b. Figures he took so long. He was always lazy and never got things done the first time.
   c. A lawyer. Wow. I wonder if he's still single.

   *Five bars does not equal five stars. If you are overly impressed by his minor achievements, you are not over him in the least.*

3. A friend told you he always talks about the funny times the two of you had at Rock Creek. You think:
   a. Was that him? Wow. That was so long ago. I thought I was there with that one guy from high school.
   b. He remembers those times? I wonder if he ever thinks about the inscription we wrote in marker under that rock. Maybe I should send him a note reminding him of it for old times' sake.
   c. I can't believe the loser used to make me go to that place. It was always cold, muddy, and full of trash. It was Rock Creek where I learned that shopping carts float.

   *If you picked "b," your emotional grip on him is far too firm. You would probably entertain the possibility of getting back together with him if the opportunity knocked.*

4. When you run into his mom in the mall, she is very cordial. She ends the conversation with a hug and a "I hope we get to see you more often." You:

a. Go home and call every friend you have in the universe trying to determine what she meant by her comment.

b. Can't remember if she's the mother of your ex from college or the one you met in Cancun.

c. Forget all about it when you see the sale sign in the window three stores down.

*If you picked "a," you might still be in love with your ex. After all, you are spending time and energy analyzing, and no diva analyzes an ex unless she cares what he thinks and feels.*

5. You're cleaning out your bedroom and you come across a box of his stuff under the bed. You:

a. Throw it in the garbage and keep cleaning.

b. Read through every note, play a CD that triggers memories, grasp his old T-shirt, and cry out, "Why did you have to leave me?"

c. Realize he always wrote the same thing in every card he ever gave you, and wonder why you didn't notice his lack of originality at the time.

*If you picked "b," you are obviously still hooked on thoughts of him and are at severe risk of a rerun.*

A rerun relationship can begin at any time and usually happens unexpectedly after you bump into him later on in life. The harder you hold on to memories of the two of you together, the more likely you'll be to give in to him if he asks you out or tries to sleep with you a year later. When you think you are completely over him, look back at this section and ask yourself again, "Am I a rerun risk?" If the answer is "yes," prepare to make a smart decision when an encounter finally happens, so you can handle it with sass.

*Good judgment comes from experience, and experience comes from bad judgment.*

—*Barry LePatner*

## The Hazards of Selective Memory

Depending on the nature of your first relationship with your ex, a rerun can be a great second chance or self-inflicted hell on earth. Sometimes relationships that are rekindled down the road turn into great romances. Other times, however, it can be like a recurring nightmare with all the old issues surfacing, and a final breakup as bad or worse than the first. To guard against the latter, recognize those factors that turn a rerun into a catastrophe.

### You Have a Selective Memory

You may have selective memory if:

* You remember the amazing time you had on the boat cruise, but not the incident at the end where he held you overboard by your arm and yelled "die, wench."
* Your friends say he was always angry, but you are certain he was merely zealous and energetic.
* You recall the long rides the two of you would take on the weekends, but you forget the time he dropped you off alongside the road and made you walk home in the dark.
* You're certain the dent in your wall is from moving the armoire, but your best friend claims your ex made it when he threw a shoe across the room.

✳  Your friends can't stand him, but you're sure it's because you only told them the bad things about your relationship.

If he didn't change at all, could you live with it? Chances are the answer is no. So a rerun relationship for those with selective memory is particularly dangerous. If you aren't sure whether or not your view has been altered by time, have a friend give her opinion on his return from the dead.

### You Have "Doormat Syndrome"

Do your friends and siblings always tell you to toughen up and be a little sassier? If you have a habit of forgiving people far too easily, you should not get involved with him again without an okay from several people you trust. Direct your attention away from rekindling the fire and focus instead on working to change your doormat status.

### You're Hooked On Old Feelings

Sometimes as months pass, a diva becomes fixated on the first few weeks of the relationship and how "into" him she felt. She convinces herself that the initial excitement was an indication that he was the right guy for her. Don't go along with a rerun relationship simply because you've had it in your head all along that you'd be lucky if he came back. Never allow your old self that was in love with him to dictate the future for the sassy new you.

### You Think He's Changed

Sometimes you might think that he's changed his ways and is back in your life for the right reasons. Explore his motivations for returning to the scene of the crime. If you think he's back with bad intentions, avoid mingling with him at all costs.

You'll know he is simply looking for easy, safe sex if:
- He calls you from his hotel room late at night when he's in town for a week.
- He looks you up right after he breaks up with a girl he's been dating and complains on the phone that he needed his freedom and missed hot women.
- He makes comments that center around your body, like "You would make a great phone sex operator," or "You would be a fabulous topless dancer."

You'll know he's after a quick ego boost if:
- He's getting in touch with you after a major letdown—he was dumped, has flunked out of school, or was fired from his job.
- He still acts like a playboy jackass and brags about all the women who love him.
- He doesn't ask you anything about you or your life. He just talks about himself.

You'll know he really is a changed man if:
- He approaches you timidly and apologizes profusely for what happened in the past, even for things you don't remember.

**Be Aware**

Keep in mind that an ex might contact you when he's in town and doesn't know anyone else, needs a place to stay, or suffers from selective memory too. Always take his return with a grain of salt until he proves himself worthy.

**Deep Diva Thought**

Think of your ex kind of like a Twinkie. Just because he's sweet and appealing at first doesn't necessarily mean he's good for you. He might have a long shelf life and still not be spoiled after ten years, but he can also make you sick with his disgusting artificial colors and flavors. Take small bites with caution until you know whether you are having a delectable treat or a disgusting concoction you should throw in the trash.

- He asks you out to dinner, picks a great place, pays in full, and is a total gentleman the entire time.
- He seems grown-up and no longer talks like a teenager in lust.
- He finally wants you to meet his parents.
- He is wearing presentable clothing for the first time in his life.

Even if you determine that he is a changed man, always approach a rerun with caution. He can be reformed but still break your heart all over again. There are lots of possible reasons why an ex returns. Consider them all and know what you're getting yourself into before you agree to give things one more go.

## Touch and Go

If you decide to give your ex a second chance, the next question you'll face is "Should I sleep with him?" Though an ex always has potential to turn into a monster when the moon is full, there are three important guidelines you can use to ensure that you make the best possible decision.

1. Be aware of the feelings sex can stir up. Think about what these feelings are and the effect they can have on you and the relationship. When you are with him you might:
   - See a bright blue Speedo and realize he only wore boxers because he knew you liked them.
   - Be forced to realize that his hard pecs are now only a memory that was frozen in time because of the breakup.
   - Come to terms with the fact that the sex you had early on in your life was not very good after all.
   - Be embarrassed because you actually believed him back then when he said he was large.
   - Deal with the fact that you have a better relationship with your dildo than you do with him.

2. Acknowledge the different types of sex with an ex and determine which will make you happy and which will not. (See extended list following.)

3. Heed the "never sleep with him if" list at all costs. Never sleep with him if:
   - You are dumping a new guy to do so.
   - You are cheating on a new guy or he's cheating on his girlfriend or wife. What goes around comes around.

*There is nothing like returning to a place that remains unchanged to find the ways in which you your-self have altered.*

*—Nelson Mandela*

*Sex without love is an empty experience, but as empty experiences go it's a pretty good one.*

—Woody Allen

- You are doing so only to prove to yourself that you're over him.
- You're doing so simply because you've been telling yourself for so long that he is what you want.
- He's been with so many girls since you broke up that chances are he has every disease in the book.
- You don't have condoms handy. Not only do you want to remain disease-free, but you also want to prevent his genes from being passed along to another generation.

### Different Types of Sex with an Ex

If the "never sleep with him if" list does not apply, and you find yourself on the brink of that magic moment, you can probably expect one of the following scenarios.

#### Steamy Bag-over-His-Head Sex

You don't miss him at all. You just think he has a hot body and you don't want to add a new guy to your roster. In fact, you hope he leaves the minute it is over because you have a nail appointment you don't want to miss. This sex is simply for the joy of it. You are 100 percent over him for good. You know there's no chance of a relapse, so you forget about who he is, the history you have, and you just have fun.

### I Miss You Sex

You are both still having second thoughts about the breakup. He thinks about you on occasion and you still sigh every now and then when you look at his picture. Now you are in the midst of reviving the relationship. Neither of you know how it is going to pan out, but it is off to a good start on the physical front and you are happy he's back.

## Why Are We Doing This Again? Sex

You immediately recall how bad he was in bed the first time around. Back then you thought it was good because you didn't know any better. Now you realize that you've grown up and you're making a big mistake by being with him again. He still hasn't learned a thing. You are wondering why you agreed to do this and you can't stop thinking about your favorite show that will be on TV when you finish.

### Drunken Sex

You can't even see who he is because things are a bit blurry, but you remember in the back of your mind that you were with an ex earlier that evening. He's drunk too, but he manages to make things happen. In the morning, you both argue about what occurred the night before. You are sure you just passed out, but he thinks that maybe you both went further. All you remember is a desperate urge to go to the bathroom, a spinning room, and a sweaty guy

When you are assessing whether or not sex with an ex is worthwhile, don't let anything fall through the cracks . . . unless of course it's him, while you're doing it on a boardwalk over the ocean.

**Sassy Scoop**

hanging over you. It was a lot like being on a really bad amusement park ride on a hot day.

### One-Way Sex

You want to get back together with him, but he is thinking "sex" and nothing else. He is a playboy and he doesn't care what girl he hurts and who he steps on in the process. You realize how selfish he is, but not until ten seconds after the whole thing is over. You give him a couple of days to rectify his behavior and treat you with respect. A week passes and you realize there is no hope. The whole thing is over for good, and he is a loser. You feel relieved to see him go.

Be sure he is doing all the right things to ensure that the type of "sex with an ex" you selected is what the experience will turn out to be. If you are reaching for good, solid "I miss you sex," make sure he builds the foundation necessary for that experience. Just like a new guy in your life, he must worship you as the sassy goddess that you are. He should be apologizing profusely for the past, and wining and dining you in the present. If you have any suspicion that he's a sex fiend on the prowl and you just happen to be in his path, by all means have dinner with him, but do not let him come over afterward. Use your intuition and don't let any wishful thinking obstruct negative signals from him. If he isn't

*One thing I've learned in all these years is not to make love when you really don't feel it; there's probably nothing worse you can do to yourself than that.*

—Norman Mailer

behaving perfectly, he does not have the right to be with the queen of sass.

Never throw out the lessons you learned from your broken heart the first time around. Make the guy do the work, ensure that he's treating you well, command respect, and do things at your own pace. Just as you apply these basic lessons to new men in your life, apply them to your ex as well. Consider him a stranger with a lot of proving to do. Don't take any chances. Make him prove himself worthy before you give him any part of you.

## The Grand Goodbye

When all is said and done, if you have determined that a rerun is not the right move to make, say your goodbyes and move on once and for all. This time around, a goodbye will be grand. You will do the honors with a handshake and a "see ya later losergator" attitude. Before you do so, don't forget to take a few things that are rightfully yours. Hopefully you still have your breakup club card. It is like a coffee club card. It is a little tally you keep in your head of the good things your ex has done for you since the horrendous breakup. He must do ten good things, each one warranting a punch . . . in the card. Then when it is completely filled up, he owes you a free latte. Until he has done ten things to make up for his asinine ways, he cannot be let off the hook for good.

*Don't have sex, man. It leads to kissing and pretty soon you have to start talking to them.*

—Steve Martin

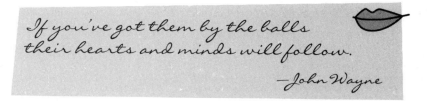

*If you've got them by the balls
their hearts and minds will follow.*

*—John Wayne*

## Things That Earn Him a Card Punch

There are plenty of ways your ex can earn his card punch. He can:

- Give you good job referrals and helpful career contacts.
- Drive you to your next destination . . . six hours away.
- Help you with a project like moving, installing an air conditioner, or carrying an entertainment center up five flights of stairs.
- Buy you lunch, dessert, and coffee at a café, and then a pair of shoes at the shop next door.
- Give you first grabs at the free concert tickets he gets through his job.
- Babysit your neurotic attack cat during all the holidays.
- Pick up your sister at the airport.
- Loan you a couple of thousand dollars for a down payment on your new yacht.
- Rewire your apartment so you can install track lighting.
- Custom-make a piece of wooden furniture to fit in your bathroom.
- Let you borrow his high-definition television the night of the big boxing match.
- Be your date for your annoying friend's wedding.

He doesn't have to fear the breakup club card. If he behaves properly, he'll pay off his debt in no time, you'll have your latte, and all will be right with the world. Then you'll have the green light to say your grand goodbye and forget he existed.

## The Goodbye

Once you're ready to say goodbye for good, there are plenty of fun ways to do the deed. This time it's your turn to show your spunky side. To have a little fun and feel vindicated for all he did, try a few of the following sassy goodbyes:

- Let him be the last to call. Then never get in touch with him again.
- Refer to your diary to find out what lines he used to initiate the break years ago. Use them on him for genuine healing.
- Sleep with him, then ask him to leave immediately. Tell him you really need your space.
- Send him an invitation for your wedding, or an e-mail mentioning your engagement.
- Have a friend call him and dump him for you.
- Send him a farewell note to the shared fax in his office.
- Forward an e-mail to all your friends letting them know it was a big mistake to get back together with him. Include him on the distribution by "accident."
- Mention you're dissing your ex to a mutual acquaintance with a big mouth. Rest assured he'll find out through her that you're breaking up with him.
- Stand him up a couple of times.
- Invite him over, shut off the lights, lie on the floor, and watch the look on his face through the sheer curtains when he realizes you're not home.
- Invite him to dinner and have another guy show up at the same time "by mistake."

The decision to get back together with an ex years later is a personal one. Most of the time it is not worth the hassle or risk. Whereas every so often a rerun relationship works out, most of the time it opens a can of worms, leaving the diva to push the squiggly pests back inside and weld the top on. If you are following the diva recovery plan you probably will not want to rekindle things anyway. Sometime in the future you will see him as an embarrassing notch in your lipstick case. However, regardless of what you do decide, proceed with caution. That way you will remain a sassy goddess with no regrets.

When you finally close the door on your ex for good, don't look back even if his leg is caught and you hear him screaming.

Sassy Scoop

*Habit is habit and not to be flung out of the window by any man, but coaxed downstairs a step at a time.*

—Mark Twain

## Chapter Nine
# The Future Is Yours

It can be difficult to think long-term after a breakup and see yourself finally over him and feeling spectacular again. The ability to see this far ahead really only comes from experience and a few strong drinks. But you have the experience behind you, and the power to pour yourself an icy cold margarita at any time. So throw a shot of optimism into that drink, put on a pair of chic sunglasses, and claim the future as your own.

### Goddess at the Wheel

A breakup can leave you feeling as if you've lost all control over your life, even those parts unrelated to your ex. But remind yourself that you have the power within you to turn your life into everything you want it to be. You've dealt with the breakup with sass; now let this quality become a fundamental part of who you are. Rediscover your personal power by living every day of your life with enthusiasm, using the essential elements of diva attitude.

### A Diva Sets Gutsy Goals

You've already accomplished short-term goals during the breakup. Maybe you cashed in your ex's belongings for the big bucks, or disconnected his hot water for a few days. Now it's time to set bigger life goals for yourself, to paint the image of the future in your mind exactly the way you want it to be. It's easy to feel overwhelmed when so many options lie before you. But don't try to do everything at once. Figure out one or two things that are important to you, and carry through until you've accomplished them.

### Start Somewhere Immediately

Turn over the list of "things I hate about my ex" and use the back to write down steps you'll take to move toward a happier future. Then start doing the things you need to do to get there. Don't sit at home waiting for the world to happen to you. You don't want to wake up twenty years from now saying "I wish I did . . . I wish I had . . ." Get going today, and live as though it's your last chance to make your dreams come true.

### Ignore the "That's Impossible" Crowd

Remember when they told you no one would believe your story about your ex's black-market office supply operation? Now he's in the slammer. Never listen to the people who tell you that something can't be done. Even if you feel confident, their negative thoughts can get in the back of your head and eat away at your will. Stay far away from anyone who exudes pessimism and a lack of enthusiasm for life.

### Remember That You Cannot Please Everyone

Live your life in the best way that you can, but don't sacrifice your own happiness while trying to make everyone else happy. Whether you're dealing with friends, children, your boss, or a man you're dating, your own fulfillment must come first. Once you're happy with your own life, you'll have more to give to those you love anyway.

### Say "No" Often, and with Diva Attitude

If you are the type of person who feels guilty when you can't help someone or when you can't complete every task you're asked to do, learn to say "no" and stick with it. Life does not reward you in direct relationship to how exhausted you are at the end of each day. Put energy toward your priorities and say "no" to everything else without feeling guilty.

### Wrestle Every Problem to the Ground

Just as you had that defensive lineman tackle your ex in the dark alley, tackle your own problems with energy and brute force. Think of solutions, pick the best one, and get going on it. Never spend time worrying about the challenges you face.

### Always Smirk or Smile

The smirk is the universal diva sign of knowledge, power, and sass. The smirk can mean any number of things, depending on how you do it and what other facial movements accompany it. Have a smirk on your face at all times so people wonder what you're thinking, why you're happy, or what you're up to. Here are a few types of sassy smirks you can use on different occasions.

### The Flirtatious Smirk

This smirk is not solely for a guy you find interesting. Use it whenever you feel playful or want something. If you're in a store and the cashier is male, flash your flirtatious smirk to get the 20-percent-off special that expired yesterday. Use this smirk at work when you need to take an extra vacation day. It is simply a smile that comes with an "I like you" facial expression, and with it you can get anything you want from anyone.

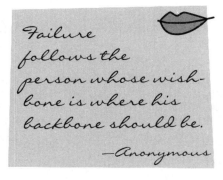

Failure follows the person whose wishbone is where his backbone should be.
—Anonymous

### The Fed-Up Smirk

Your dry cleaning is messed up for the third time and you have to take it back in and have it done again. You want to complain without coming off like a scary wench. Use the fed-up smirk to deliver a sugar-covered punch to the man behind the desk. As you ask him to redo the items and return your cash, keep the fed-up smirk glued to your face. You catch more flies with honey, but even more with a honey-coated swatter.

### Smirk of Disbelief

Your coworker hasn't shut up all day and now you're in a meeting and he's even worse. Flash your smirk of disbelief his way, sending a strong "Are you kidding me? Aren't you ever going to shut up?" message. Shake your head along with it, roll your eyes, and then sigh heavily. If this smirk doesn't quiet him down, seal his mouth shut with packing tape.

### Default Smirk

The default smirk is one you have on your face every day when you are walking down the street. Check out other people and pay close attention to the ones who scowl when they are doing nothing more than sitting on a bus or train. They usually have a negative vibe surrounding them, and you can tell they are unhappy. Never let your default facial expression be an unhappy one. Replace it with the default smirk of a dazzling diva.

## Beef Up Your Attitude

Approach every situation with a healthy dose of confidence, enthusiasm, and spirit. Toss out a playful remark when someone is bugging you. Walk and talk like you own the room. Laugh whenever you can. Throughout your life, you will always have an edge if you have a positive attitude and a mischievous spirit. Believe that you deserve respect and that you already have what it takes to do the things you want to do. Don't be afraid to ask for what you want. Believe that you are a worthy diva, and the world will be yours.

### Be a Decisive Diva

Remember that indecision makes progress impossible. Don't spend hours comparing shoes on the rack and calling every friend to ask them which ones you should buy. Just purchase the pair you like best and move on. Time spent fretting over the decision can be better spent finding a cute skirt to go with the shoes.

*If you are going to wait for someone to encourage you to do something, you just better give it up.*

*—Cher*

## Copycat Courage

When a soldier goes into battle, she always studies the opponent and tries to understand his strategy. Once she does, her knowledge coupled with her own strengths makes her invincible. Though men are not the enemy (though some come close), study them as if they are. For hundreds of years they have believed it is their right to take control and reach for the stars. Women, on the other hand, have had a tougher row to hoe, overcoming the "weak, submissive" stereotype to become the sassy, take-charge superstars we are today. Even now, a small ripple of archaic male chauvinism can make its way to the back of the female mind and undermine a diva's rise to the top. Many women still grow up a step behind their male counterparts in the gumption, gall, and "I can have it all" mindset. Instead of blaming the guys for the centuries of training they bring to the table, we can learn from them (and then overtake them if we wish). Incorporate lessons from the other side into your sassy strategy.

### Make a Muscle

Men never think their arm muscles are too small to pull up a sleeve and flex at a party. Don't be afraid to pat yourself on the back for your own strengths. Show them off and let people know you've got what it takes to deal with anything that comes your way.

### Fight When Necessary

At the very least, signal in some way that you disagree. Don't be afraid to show how you really feel about something. Assert your will with gusto.

### Go Golfing

Or go shopping or take a day trip with other women just to connect, talk, and make the contacts you need for your career and happiness. Men never hesitate to drop everything for a game of golf. Call in sick and hit the stores. You can carry around the golf club in case you run into your ex, but never, ever wear the plaid shorts and white socks.

### Spit, Burp, and . . .

Okay, you don't have to go that far, but be proud of your body. Men seem to grow up amused by their own bodies, even the completely disgusting parts. If they can do it, so can divas everywhere.

### Act Like You Know Everything

Even when you don't. Men always seem to have answers in meetings, in conversation, and any time they are asked a big question. This habit of theirs makes them seem sharp and confident to

*When I eventually met Mr. Right I had no idea that his first name was Always.*

*—Rita Rudner*

those around them, even when they are not. You can give off your own air of confidence by following their lead and showing what you know to the world.

### Search for the Remote

Most men would rather watch *Mister Rogers* reruns than get up and change the channel manually. Unlike women, who will tackle anything with stamina, many men are programmed to look for the easiest way to accomplish a task. When the result is more important than the process, take a clue from the guys. Keep the remote at hand and save yourself the extra trips across the room.

### Let the Bathroom Get Dirty

Many women still feel responsible for keeping their house or apartment looking perfect. Don't let traditional beliefs back you into a corner with a mop. Adopt the mentality of a guy every now and then. Let things go, and spend the time doing something else. Sit down, relax, and have a cup of coffee instead of straightening up your place. Or go out and play for a while. That's what the guys do.

### Surround Yourself with Girls

It's important enough to say a hundred times—always have good girlfriends in your life, and make time to do things with them regardless of who you are dating. A man will never fulfill every need you have, even if he is one you manufactured with electronic parts left over from your ex's favorite gadgets. Surround yourself with girls, enjoy their company, and share the trials and tribulations of being fabulous.

## *Love the Game*

Men seem to be obsessed with sports of one kind or another. Their competitive mentality carries over into their work and personal life. While you don't have to become an armchair quarterback with a beer belly, learn to think of life as a game. Then have fun playing it.

## *Idolize a Role Model*

Emulate the style and attitude of women you admire. Let the "Old Divas Network" guide you to success in your life. Read about and study influential women and watch the way they handle life's challenges.

You can be a goddess at the wheel and steer your life in the direction you wish it to go if you learn from your own experiences and from the experiences of those around you. Take control of your world and tackle everything that comes your way with confidence and attitude. Continually combine new knowledge with your existing talents and you will be a lean, mean diva machine.

## Divas in History

History is laden with brave, sassy women who made their mark despite the restrictions of their time and culture. Remember and study these women, because they paved the way for divas everywhere to be free superstars. Even if you don't agree with their beliefs or pursuits, study them and respect them for their confidence, bravery, and spunk. Emulate their strengths, learn from their weaknesses, and soon you'll be the diva role model everyone admires.

## *Queen Elizabeth the First (1533–1603)*

She ruled England during "The Golden Age." Well known as a masterful politician and negotiator, it is rumored she used her single state as a weapon, luring enemies under the guise of marriage or scaring them by threatening to marry their enemies. She once told her only love interest, Robert Dudley, "You are like my little dog; when people see you they know I am nearby."

## *Abigail Adams (1744–1818)*

Witty, self-educated, and sassy, she coached John Adams as he worked to form a new nation in the early days of the Republic. Famous for her mischievous and opinionated letters to her husband, she once wrote, "If particular care and attention is not paid to the ladies, we are determined to foment a rebellion, and will not hold ourselves bound by any laws in which we have no voice, or representation."

## *Dorothy Parker (1893–1967)*

A talented and spirited writer, she composed numerous articles, poems, and stories that celebrate sass. She had a gift for identifying the idiosyncrasies of human nature. When she learned that Calvin Coolidge was dead, she asked, "How could they tell?"

## *Bette Davis (1908–1989)*

An actress with incredible range, she was well known for being strong-minded and witty. Though not considered conventionally attractive, she became a sensation through hard work, nerve, and spunk. When talking about her fourth husband, she said, "Gary was a macho man, but none of my husbands was ever man enough to become Mr. Bette Davis."

### Eva Perón (1919–1952)

She became First Lady of Argentina, despite being born into poverty. Powerful, intelligent, and shrewd, she was loved by the people of her country. She believed that "Without fanaticism one cannot accomplish anything."

### Lauren Bacall (1924– )

A famed Hollywood actress from the Golden Era of Hollywood, she is said to have a talent for turning the most powerful men into her followers. When speaking of her marriage to Humphrey Bogart, she said, "Overjoyed as I was to be Mrs. Bogart, I had no intention of allowing Miss Bacall to slide into oblivion."

### Margaret Thatcher (1925– )

Britain's first female prime minister, she was also the first in the twentieth century to win three consecutive general elections. She showed her sass when she said, "I am extraordinarily patient, provided I get my own way in the end."

### Barbra Streisand (1942– )

She bucked the rock 'n' roll trend for years and stayed true to her own musical style. As a successful, strong, and incredibly talented singer and actress, she once asked, "Why is it men are permitted to be obsessed about their work, but women are only permitted to be obsessed about men?"

### Cher (1946– )

Cher is proof that women do get better with age. She is famous for her musical talent, attitude, and spunk. She once said, "Yes, it's a man's world, but that's all right because they're making a total mess of it. We're chipping away at their control, taking the parts we want. Some women think it's a difficult task, but it's not."

### Oprah Winfrey (1954– )

One of the most charismatic and popular modern-day celebrities, she is a role model for all women, radiating confidence, attitude, and integrity. She exuded sass when she said, "Think like a queen. A queen is not afraid to fail. Failure is another steppingstone to greatness."

Throughout history there have been amazing female spies and military officers. Many women held other traditionally male positions, sometimes working without the benefit of the formal title or rewards that should have accompanied their jobs. Many of these women weren't recognized until years later, when historians explored their work. If you are looking for fascinating, gutsy role models to give you sassy inspiration, read about Dr. Mary E. Walker, Lt. Annie G. Fox, Lydia Barrington Darragh, Sarah Bradlee Fulton, and Elizabeth Van Lew. These are just a few of the many sassy women in history.

The diva role model you choose might be a woman in your life, a friend, a coworker, or a famous person not listed here. They aren't superwomen; they're simply women who overcame obstacles, criticism, or cultural bias to be true to their sassy side. Follow their lead and take the reins in your own life. Be true to who you are, and cultivate the attitude necessary to follow your dreams.

## Situational Sass

Every day you will walk out into the world and face many situations that put your spunk to the test. Though you can't prepare for them all, you can make yourself aware of the common ones and have an action plan ready when they pop up. Some of the more common times that call for situational sass are listed here, along with appropriately spirited actions to deal with them.

**Situation:** You take your car into a repair shop and the con man behind the counter tries to sell you hubcaps that double as stereo speakers.

**Sassy move:** Do your homework before setting foot in any automotive or hardware shop. Prove to them that you know your stuff by tossing around a few phrases like "neoprene gasket" or "driveshaft yoke." Make up your own phrase just for fun. "I hear a murmur in my Prada-belt."

**Situation:** You're in a work meeting and every time someone asks you a question, your boss answers for you.

**Sassy move:** Interrupt the wench when she takes the floor. Of course, you risk ticking her off, but perhaps one time is all it will take to make her shut her trap.

**Situation:** You're in a public place and the line for the women's restroom is out the door and around the block.

**Sassy move:** Flip the "M" upside down and claim the men's room as your own. A sassy diva never waits in line for bathrooms, bars, or boys.

**Situation:** The new guy you're dating wants you to wear lacy undergarments every day despite the fact that they are itchy and impractical.
**Sassy move:** Sew him a pair of lace-lined boxers and tell him you'll abide by his rule if he does the same.

**Situation:** You are tired of carrying a handbag everywhere you go and worrying about losing it, but when you put things in your pockets, your hips look like they've grown 10 inches.
**Sassy move:** Give yourself a purse-free boob job. Stick some cash and a bank card in one side of your bra, your keys in the other. There's nothing wrong with a little extra padding for a legitimate reason.

Wherever you are and whatever the situation, always have on hand quick comebacks, sassy smirks, and insolent moves. Embrace your personal power and stand up for yourself with attitude. The more you practice this mindset, the easier it will become to think on your feet and deal like a diva. Soon it will be second nature, and you'll fly full speed ahead toward stardom.

*Every Independent Diva Should . . .*

- Live on her own for a while before moving in with a significant other.
- Know how to change a tire (and how to talk any guy into doing it for her for free).
- Understand how to work a power drill and other fix-it tools.

- Take a self-defense class once every few years (and practice the moves on her ex).
- Open her own bank account and develop good credit.
- Understand the basics of investing and build her own portfolio.
- Feel comfortable traveling alone and navigating a new city.
- Complete her education and develop a marketable job skill.
- Keep in touch with at least one male friend who worships her.
- Have at least one female friend who she can ask for help in any situation.
- Have at least one ex she used to be in love with who now makes her cringe.
- Have a picture that reminds her of how far she's come since she was in high school, and a current one that she will be able to look back at in five years.

# Chapter Ten
# Diva Debut

Though you are focused now on your own life and happiness, chances are you will begin to find men interesting again at some point. When an amusing guy does stumble down your path, you will be more ready than ever to make your debut onto the dating scene with sass and style.

As an independent diva, your job is to have some fun and date with a carefree attitude. You'll soon discover that boys are toys put on the earth to amuse you, befriend you, and ideally, to buy you free drinks and dinners until they've proven their worth. In the process, you might find one you like and decide to invest in the entire package. Until then, the dating scene is a party full of different types of treats. Find those that are cheesy, sweet, or simply delicious. Then dig in.

## Bad Boys Be Gone

Men can be bastards. There's no doubt about that. But if your breakup has you packing for the convent, take a step back and

*I love men, even though they're lying, cheating scumbags.*

—Gwyneth Paltrow

assess the situation again. It is perfectly okay to decide that dating is not for you right now. Your life is about your happiness, not about meeting a man. But make sure that whatever decision you make is an active one, not a road you choose solely because you're angry or afraid of being hurt again.

### The Good Things about Guys

To keep yourself in the right carefree mindset, take a moment to remember all the good things about guys. Keep the list on hand so you never fall into "I hate men" mode and become Sister Diva against your will.

*Not all men . . .*
- Are serial killers
- Celebrate Super Bowl Sunday as a national holiday
- Would vote Pamela Anderson to be the first female president
- Still play the *Rocky* soundtrack when they work out
- Think a hamburger and fries do a romantic dinner make
- Wear T-shirts with yellow armpit stains
- Believe communication is responding "yes" or "no"

*At least one man out there . . .*
- Is CEO of a major chocolate company
- Tracks birthdays and anniversaries with his Palm Pilot
- Is very handsome, chivalrous, and mute
- Owns a vacuum cleaner and knows how to use it

- Knows Dorothy would have made it to Oz just fine on her own
- Wears stylish clothes and yet remains heterosexual
- Would rather watch a documentary than late-night porn (or at least pretends he would)
- Has already been beaten into shape by a diva mom or sister

Remember: Men might share the same basic anatomy, but they don't share the same brain or personality. New guys you meet will have a better brain, a better personality, and if you're really lucky, a better anatomy too. Not all men are bastards. Rumor has it that there is at least one out there who isn't. If we all band together, maybe we can find him and live happily ever after in a polygamous household filled with chocolate and designer handbags. Better yet, maybe we will find more than one good one. They are out there, but you have to dig deep because they are hidden from view by the ubiquitous jackass population. It's hard to shoot a duck when it's surrounded by turkeys.

> If you drank a smoothie made with spoiled milk, you wouldn't swear off all smoothies for the rest of your life. And like this cool, fruity drink, a bad experience with a rotten man should not prevent you from going for the sweet and tasty variety in the future.
>
> Sassy Scoop

### Love Artist or Con Artist?

Before you even consider making a debut onto the dating scene, learn to identify a bad purchase before you buy. It can take weeks for an "appears to be decent" guy to show his true colors, but you can weed out the really scary ones by paying close attention to a guy's appearance and behavior right away. Is he a love artist or a con artist? Identify a bad guy quickly by following these guidelines.

*The bad guy:*

- Is dressed like he hasn't done laundry in weeks.
- Is sporting an "I'm a cult member" haircut and weird symbolic pins on his jacket.
- Pays for everything with cash and uses a pseudonym.
- Doesn't have a photo ID or looks nothing like the blond woman in the one he's using.
- Has a bad relationship or no relationship with all members of his immediate family.
- Moves his hands nonchalantly into places where they shouldn't be.
- Makes suggestive remarks and invites you up to his place right away.
- Goes out of town constantly and won't say where he's going.
- Claims he's not married but has women's clothes and jewelry in his bedroom.
- Tells you right away that he wants you to stay home and bear his eight children.
- Tells you right away that he wants you to support him financially.
- Calls you "little lady," "little girl," "baby," or other equally creepy and demeaning terms.
- Takes you to a drive-through on your first date and says, "We have to keep moving."
- Has more snakes on his skin than are in the lizard exhibit at the zoo.
- Has more piercing holes than your pasta strainer.
- Wants to take you on a surprise vacation after your second date.

> *The perfect lover is one who turns into pizza at 4 a.m.*
>
> —*Charles Pierce*

- Wants you to go for a drive with him down a dark country road the night you meet him.
- Carries a pick, a shovel, and other suspicious materials in the back of his car.

*Particularly, beware of the guy who:*
- Cares more about his cell phone than he does about you.
- Has a mullet and really bad teeth.
- Is unemployed with no job search plans in sight.
- Lives with more than a few well-kept pets in his apartment.
- Lives with his parents for absolutely no good reason.
- Has several ex-girlfriends, all with unlisted phone numbers.

## Lessons from the Dressing Room

You are now equipped to weed out any slimy guy who comes your way, and you feel ready to date like a fiend. Fortunately, everything a diva needs to know about dating she learned in a trendy boutique dressing room: Always have several pieces to choose from. Never make an important decision when you have PMS. A dress that looks beautiful in the window can turn out to be a really bad fit.

Swear off any guys who give you a queasy feeling. As a rule, you should not date someone who makes you feel like you're going to puke.

Sassy Scoop

Take time to review these dressing-room lessons. They're critical to having diva power on the dating scene.

### *Lesson #1: Variety Makes a Wardrobe Fabulous*

Variety is the key to a spectacular wardrobe, so you take extra pains to have many colors and styles represented. This rule also applies to your portfolio of men. If you have historically filled your man stash with guys of one kind, it is time to branch out and include a few new ones. It's easy to get hung up on a certain type, one distinguished by his physical attributes, mental faculties (though that's a little farfetched), or unique style. Old habits die hard. But remember that your judgment years ago, when you became addicted to this breed, might not have been as good as it is today. If you have any doubt, pull out old pictures and look at your hair at the time. That should sober you up. Keep an assortment of men at your disposal, one appropriate for every mood and season. Only by doing so will your knowledge of the man market grow—and knowledge, my dear, is diva power.

### *Lesson #2: Some Dresses Look Better On*

You see a wrinkled red piece of cloth on a hanger and cringe, but it's your size and it's marked 50 percent off, so you decide you might as well try it on. Once you pull it over your head, you see that the little ragged piece actually has Saturday night potential.

*Insanity: doing the same thing over and over again and expecting different results.*

*—Albert Einstein*

Another lesson from the dressing room—just like dresses, some guys look better on. Sometimes your instincts can be off, but with men you don't have the "sale" sign egging you on to give him a second chance. Unless your instincts are screaming "this man will bury you under the floorboards," there are certain types of guys that might be worth a second look. Here are a few.

### The First-Date Disaster

He steps in dog doo on the way to the restaurant. You drink the olive oil, thinking it is water. Lots of weird things happen when two people meet up for the first time in an unfamiliar place and try to make small talk for hours on end. If he smiles at you all night and stares into your eyes like his face is frozen, he might be a nut job. But if you leave thinking he's normal and you had fun but you just aren't sure, give the guy a second chance.

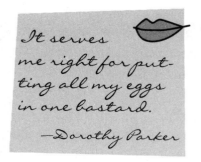

*It serves me right for putting all my eggs in one bastard.*
*—Dorothy Parker*

### The Quiet Guy

Some guys seem quiet on a first date but six months later you can't get them to tone down their behavior long enough to get through a civilized meal. Just as divas have "off nights," so do men. If his quiet nature is the main thing about him that turns you off, give it a go again, and throw in a few really strong drinks next time.

### The Poor Dresser

Men are notoriously bad dressers, but some are worse than others. If you're throwing out a guy just because he wears a super-starched blue shirt and khakis (a.k.a. the man uniform) every day of his life, remember that you will have plenty of influence over his wardrobe in the near future.

### The Slightly Nerdy Guy

Nerdy guys have learned to compensate for their lack of studliness by being funnier, kinder, and more interesting than traditionally "cool" men. Nerdy guys also typically make a higher salary than their cool counterparts. Pass up a nerdy opportunity and you might miss out on the one guy who can really round out your man stash.

If you're dating with a carefree attitude, you shouldn't be making snap decisions anyway. Give lots of guys a chance just to have fun and see what's out there. The more guys you have in your life, the less influence any one guy will have over you. The ultimate feeling of diva power will come when you can tell any unseemly character goodbye without flinching. Only those who are worthy belong in the front of your closet.

## Lesson #3: A "Safety" Is Not the Best You Can Do

You always have the little black dress you can wear at the drop of a hat. But it is not the beautiful ensemble that will make you the belle of the ball. A "safety spouse" is just like the little black dress. He's reliable, he fits well, and he's a great backup. But he's not exactly what you need to be fabulous. A safety spouse might be a friend, coworker, or an ex. He is whatever guy you think you "can marry in five years if you don't meet anyone you like better." It's time to get rid of your safety spouse and open up to finding the perfect flattering alternative. He's all right to keep around in case you need a last-minute party date, but he's no match for the slinky number that will complement your incredible style.

*Lesson #4: Spectacular outfits are often the least difficult to put together*

You're trying to get ready for a big night out and the clothes continue to pile up, dress upon skirt, shirt upon pants, until the pile hits the ceiling. It seems like the more effort you put into finding the right outfit, the harder it gets. The same is true with men, of course, but the pile consists of pieces like these:

- Calling him too frequently.
- Staying on the phone too long.
- Filling every moment of silence with "What are you thinking?"
- Asking him pointed questions like "Where were you last night? Why didn't you call me?"
- Making self-deprecating remarks about your looks, intelligence, or abilities.
- Acting threatened by other women, especially his women friends.
- Putting down other women in front of him (unless those tramps deserve it).
- Inviting him on a trip to Europe or a weekend in New England when you've only been dating for three days.
- Telling him about every problem, issue, and bad relationship you've ever had.
- Sleeping with him too soon.
- Taking his words and actions too seriously in the first few months of dating.
- Telling him you think he's "the one" and you've told your parents about him.
- Wallpapering your room with his picture.

*The male is a domestic animal which, if treated with firmness, can be trained to do most things.*

*—Jilly Cooper*

All the effort you exert trying to put together the right outfit usually results in one that is still not quite what you wanted. So you resolve to shop again in the near future. Remember this lesson and approach every guy with a laid-back, cool diva attitude. Never keep a guy around if he requires too much work. You need your energy for more important things, like traveling to your masseuse. And remember that Sunday always rolls around—you slip on the first thing you find in your closet and walk out feeling like a million bucks. That one piece gets more wear than all the difficult ensembles combined. A guy worth having will only take a couple of minutes to whip into shape, and he'll be around for a while (or at least until you get sick of him!).

## Lesson #5: If It's Flawed, Return It Promptly

You never keep a purchase around if it has a hole in it or it just doesn't fit right. You take it back, get a refund, and look for a suitable replacement. Likewise, there's no point in holding on to a guy who is just not worth it. Fifty years ago, a girl's father would chase after a guy with a shotgun if he did something wrong. A good dad chased every suitor once or twice just to scare him.

**Sassy Scoop**
Please don't feed the ego. It might bite you.

**Keep Only the Best**
A goddess can't afford to have her wardrobe corrupted by an ugly, ill-fitting item of cheap quality. Each piece must emanate style and enhance the natural beauty of the wearer.

Today things are different. A diva does away with the bad guy herself and her parents don't even know she was dating him until they hear about the accident on the evening news. It's up to you to decide what behavior is acceptable and which actions warrant lifelong anguish and torture. So set your own standards high and never hesitate to take back any purchase that doesn't live up to your expectations.

### Lesson #6: Every Now and Then, Throw on Old Comfy Jeans

A spectacular dress or tailored pantsuit can make you feel like you just stepped off a runway, but every now and then it's good to set those items aside and dig out the old comfy jeans from the back of your closet. Your friends are like these old, faithful pieces of your wardrobe. It can be difficult to resist a Friday night with a studly guy when he tells you he's home watching an intelligent program on the women's suffrage

Tell a guy that you don't want to go on another date using the words of Groucho Marx, "I've had a perfectly wonderful evening. But this wasn't it."

Sassy Scoop

movement (or more likely, some cheesy dating game). But keep in mind that there are certain days when he is just not the appropriate thing to wear. And if he does go out of style, it can take a while to find another piece worth buying. So have a jeans day every now and then. They look great in every season, they're always in vogue, and they can last years longer than so many other purchases.

The lessons you learn from the dressing room are critical to dating like a diva. Keep them in mind as you make your way onto the scene again and you'll pull together a man stash that contains a perfect pick for every occasion.

## Is He Worthy?

If you do find one particular guy who is normal, seems clean, and has a little bit of potential above and beyond the others, don't forget to ask yourself the most important question: Is he worthy? As you evaluate his candidacy, try to remember your jackass ex and the experience you had with him. Apply the knowledge you acquired to your new situation. To determine whether or not a guy is even in the game, answer the following questions.

**Don't Get Hooked on the High**

If you enjoy the thrill of the chase but get bored with the prize, be careful you don't ditch a guy simply because the initial dating high has passed. The surefire way to end up with the wrong guy is to blow off all the right ones that come your way.

# Quiz
## Does He Deserve a Diva Like You?

1. Your parents are coming into town and they offer to take the two of you out to dinner. Your new guy:
   a. Leaves that morning on an emergency flight to Japan.
   b. Suggests a local place called "Eats," and laughs when your mom cringes at the scary regulars.
   c. Picks a fantastic restaurant, foots the bill, and schedules a fishing trip with your talk-aholic father.

   *The only right answer is "c." If he doesn't make an effort with your family and friends, he is clearly not worthy of your time. Give him the boot.*

2. You've been dying to see a new movie that's out, and you invite him to go along. It's not really his thing. He:
   a. Tells you how wrong you are about the flick and tries to convince you to see *Revenge of the Mullet Men* instead.
   b. Surprises you with tickets and makes a reservation at a nearby dessert place for right after the film.
   c. Suddenly has an important Friday night work meeting with a major client.

   *The correct answer is "b." If he doesn't prioritize your interests, he is not properly worshiping you. He deserves nothing other than a swift goodbye (after a surprise trip to a chick-flick movie marathon, of course).*

3. You're driving home at night on a dark road when a rain storm hits and you can't see three feet in front of the car. He:
   a. Screams at you that it's your fault for planning the trip to begin with.

b. Drives two miles per hour while yelling every curse word on the planet.

c. Pulls off the road, finds a cozy bed and breakfast, and makes you laugh for the rest of the night with multiple renditions of "Singing in the Rain."

*The answer is "c." A candidate worth keeping around will make you laugh even in the most difficult situations. A sense of humor is crucial to relationship survival. If he doesn't have one, throw him out into the storm and lock the door for good.*

4. It's your anniversary. He:
   a. Creates a cute calendar out of a sentimental picture, brings you roses, and thanks you for putting up with him for another year.
   b. Calls you from a bar to remind you to tape the big game.
   c. Gives you the same card he gave you last year, with Wite-Out smeared over the date.

*Choice "a." is the only acceptable answer. No guy worth his weight in diamonds will forget an important holiday, your birthday, or your anniversary. These dates should be as special to him as they are to you.*

5. He tells you his new assistant is a twenty-two-year-old blond bombshell. You:
   a. Forget all about it until you stop by his office six months later and see the mailroom guy ogling her.
   b. Wonder whether or not she is assisting him in other ways every night that he works late.
   c. Know her entire life story within three weeks because he won't stop talking about her.

*The only right answer is "a." Trust is a critical part of a rela-*
*tionship. If you feel like he can't be trusted and you consider*
*yourself to be fairly laid back, get rid of him promptly. There's*
*no time to waste on guys who lack integrity.*

Have your own list of critical qualities on hand to evaluate
any guy at any time. Evaluate a man like an expensive piece of
jewelry: you have to know how
to identify the good ones so
your man stash is made up of
only the most worthy pieces.
In addition to the qualities
highlighted in the previous
quiz, consider his sense of
commitment, willingness to
cooperate, enthusiasm, matu-
rity level, and anything else
you deem important. Evaluate
any guy who comes your way,
so you never waste your time
on a cheap fake that turns
your skin green.

Good looks and a great bod are
excellent features in any
specimen of male. Keep in mind,
however, that these features do
not make or break a worthy
candidate. Decide to buy based
on less ephemeral criteria. If he
does happen to be good looking
as well, consider it a
free gift with
purchase.

Sassy
Scoop

*Men are like fine wine. They all
start out like grapes, and it's our
job to stomp on them and keep them in
the dark until they mature into something we'd like to have dinner with.*

*—Anonymous*

## The Dating Diet

If you do determine that a guy is worthy enough to be an exclusive beau, start out the relationship on the right foot by instituting an approach to dating that's a lot like a diet. Diets are usually hell to stick to, but in the end, they pay off. The diet approach to dating has the same requirements as a regular diet: willpower, self-restraint, and patience. The only difference is that in the dating diet, your new boy toy is that big piece of chocolate cake, and your independent diva lifestyle is a healthful, nutritious salad. Just as a regular diet rests on the idea of nutritional balance, the dating diet is based on the premise that a woman will have better, longer-lasting relationships if she maintains a balance of her "guy life" and "diva life." The dating diet will help you do just that. The plan is simple.

### Restrict Your Intake of Chocolate Cake

When you catch yourself falling prey to the wiles of a new love interest, remember that you are still an independent goddess. Never ditch your diva life and jump full force into social hibernation with a new beau. Have a bite of dessert once or twice a week, and then balance it out with good, nutritious portions of sassy living.

*This guy says, "I'm perfect for you, because I'm a cross between a macho and a sensitive man." I said, "Oh, a gay trucker?"*

—Judy Tenuta

## Know Your Weaknesses

If you always cheat on your diet on weekends, i.e., spend far too much time with him, be aware of this weakness and work extra hard during those times to curb your appetite. Have a plan to go out with your glam posse at least one night every weekend, or pull a few friends onboard who are in the same situation and form a dating diet group. If you do break down, stand right back up in your cute heels and keep going.

## Fight Cravings

Don't go for weeks without a little taste of dessert and then go crazy and binge for three days. See him in small increments more frequently to fight off cravings. Better to see him several times for a half-hour than to spend four days straight with him and allow him into every nook and cranny of your world too early on.

## Don't Expect Results Too Soon

Diets take time to work, and no one achieves results overnight.

Remember that dating begins as a game made up of complex factors like attitude, banter, emotion, and ego. Have patience and play along with things. Never try to force the diet to work faster.

## Don't Weigh Yourself Too Often

Don't worry about how you're doing. Assume that you're doing great simply because you are a brilliant superstar. You will know how things are going when he falls at your feet and declares his undying love. Until then, don't think about your progress. Just have fun and do your best to balance guy life and diva life.

### Stay Active and Energetic

No diet is complete without a regular dose of activity. Keep busy, continue to exercise, and fill up your days with fun times on your own or with your glam posse. Never get into the habit of "dinner and a movie" every night of your life with Mr. Chocolate Cake. Move and groove even more when you're on the dating diet.

You cannot go cold turkey and adopt all new habits overnight. However, as you integrate your diva self with your dating self, the concept of "balance" will start to feel like second nature. Once it feels natural, you can loosen up a little and put the diet plan back in the closet. However, begin by eating chocolate cake in moderation. "Everything in moderation" is the essence of an effective diet and a healthy love life.

### The Fickle Seasons on Planet Love

If a guy makes his way into the man stash and then past the early stages of the dating diet, you will have to decide whether or not you want to promote him to a more serious level in your love life. From start to finish, you will encounter ups and downs in the relationship. These fickle seasons of love are important to understand so you'll know what to expect and will have the proper gear in place. Otherwise, you might be taken by surprise and replace a guy based on a false alarm. Deciding whether or not to keep a guy around is a bit more complex than making the initial "is he worthy of another date" decision. But understanding love's fickle

*Marriage has no guarantees. If that's what you're looking for, go live with a car battery.*

—Erma Bombeck

seasons will help you evaluate him on an ongoing basis with a trained eye.

There are five seasons on planet love.

### Spring

You meet and you're in mad, passionate love. It's "love at first sight." Your hormones take over like a drug and prevent you from seeing anything bad about your perfect new boy toy. His extra pounds are cute; his music taste, divine. Life is as close as it gets to heaven on earth.

### Summer

The relationship is heated and going strong. You're sure he's "the one." You tell all your friends to get out their bridesmaids dresses, and you book a reception hall. You are the envy of all couples you know because you have the perfect relationship.

### Fall

Things suddenly start falling apart. The two of you are fighting, and the relationship is not as blissful as it once was. Hormones have worn off, and the flaws they disguised are staring you down. You hate the way he clanks the spoon on the side of his mug when he stirs his coffee. He can't stand the way you thump your feet against the hardwood floor. You're just not sure if this guy is really right for you after all.

### Winter

The passionate attraction cools off, but so do the arguments. You decide to stay together and you're learning to live with each other's idiosyncrasies. Your relationship is one of stability, intimacy, and cooperation. Though you still love one another, it is a different kind of love.

### Monsoon Season

This season is a special one reserved for couples that decide to break up. Neither of you has any problem pouring forth your own reasons for going through with the split. The good news is that once the rain has passed, springtime with a new man will be on its way again.

The bottom line is that every relationship has challenges, even if the guy has perfect scores in the worthiness category. All couples face issues they must work through. It is important to separate deal-breakers from the little things that can be resolved. Divorce statistics are high in part because many people bail during the "fall" apart season. They view their petty arguments as a sign that the end is inevitable. The truth is, however, that every relationship is ridden with obstacles that couples must work to overcome, and doing so only raises the level of intimacy between two people. Be aware of the fickle seasons on planet love and keep them in mind as you evaluate the relationships that come your way.

I think men who have a pierced ear are better prepared for marriage. They've experienced pain and bought jewelry.

—Rita Rudner

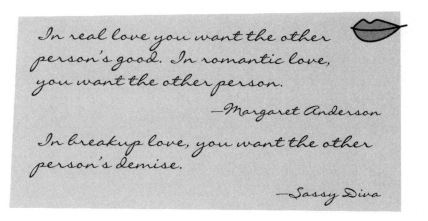

In real love you want the other person's good. In romantic love, you want the other person.

—Margaret Anderson

In breakup love, you want the other person's demise.

—Sassy Diva

## Forever Divalicious

You've come full circle and you're back in the swing of life. You're through with your ex, you're dating new guys, and you're having a blast. Or you're taking a break from the dating world for a while and focusing on your own rise to power. Whatever you decide to do from this point forward, you will do it as the sassy diva you were born to be. You are forever fabulous and yum . . . yum . . . yum . . . divalicious.

You know you're divalicious because:

### You're over the Jackass

You are *so* over him, in fact, that you are kind of embarrassed to admit you dated him. You feel sorry for any girl who ends up in his line of fire, because he's a heck of a lot more trouble than he's worth. You are showing all the signs of a goddess who just doesn't care if he lives or dies. You:

- Can eat a meal, dessert, and an ice-cream shake in one sitting, with no thoughts of him to make your stomach churn.

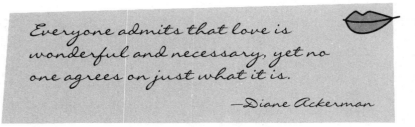

*Everyone admits that love is wonderful and necessary, yet no one agrees on just what it is.*

—Diane Ackerman

- Think all the guys you meet are better than he was in some way.
- Sold all his stuff on the Internet, shipped it rush delivery, and bought yourself a hot pink boa with the cash.
- Have stopped breaking into his e-mail account and signing him up for promotions.
- Took down the gay pride banner you draped across his car when his Bible-Belt parents came to visit.
- Replaced his name in "emergency contact" with a good gal pal's.
- See him out on weekends and take pity on the girls he's talking to.
- Can't remember his phone number for the life of you.

You're feeling sassy. You couldn't care less if he falls off the face of the earth tomorrow. Closure came when you couldn't remember his name. If you aren't quite there yet, you will be before long, because you are destined to be forever divalicious.

### You're Having Some Fun Showcasing a New Beau

You have one boy toy in your man stash worth flaunting on your arm. He's your trophy guy, and you have some fun showing him off. You don't really care what your ex thinks, but it is kind of fun to do a little needling.

- Let your new beau lick mousse off your fingers when you're seated in your ex's favorite restaurant.
- Send your new guy by his place to return that old sweatshirt you found under the bed.
- Forget to eliminate his name from the list of guests for your new guy's birthday party.
- Prepare for the inevitable "please come back to me" call by having your phone forwarded to your new guy's cell phone.
- Invite him to your wedding(s). Seat him with your other exes and sprinkle the table with flyers detailing a recommended monetary gift.

The fun doesn't have to end because the relationship did. Exes exist for a reason—to provide divas everywhere with years of laughter and fun stories. Have a ball with your new life and sassy attitude. You deserve to. You are forever divalicious.

Send your ex a different self-help gift every year. When he gets older and starts to fall apart, pick up the pace.

Sassy Scoop

## *You're Feeling Ready to Impart the Diva Way*

By now you feel so confident that you want to impart your knowledge to fellow divas and men alike. You are a glowing example of wit, class, and unparalleled sass. You are a walking, breathing example of delicious divadom. You:

- Cop a little attitude when someone asks you to do something you don't want to do.
- Tackle everything with enthusiasm and optimism.

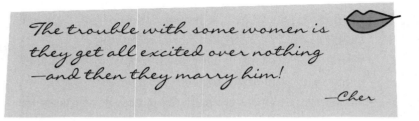

*The trouble with some women is they get all excited over nothing—and then they marry him!*

—Cher

- Live your life independently, even when you're sharing it with a guy.
- Put your father, brother, uncles, male coworkers, and friends in their place when they toss out chauvinistic remarks.
- Make men fall at your feet, and then do with them what you please.
- Know that the world is yours and your future will be whatever you want it to be.

Divalicious is an attitude that permeates your life. You are a role model of strength and cunning, wit and charm, success and sauciness. No lame guy who crosses your path has a chance in hell of survival. You are a diva to die for, and you know it!

# Conclusion

The divine goddess of retribution watches over women everywhere and avenges them against lovers gone wrong. This mythical figure is a part of stories passed down through the ages by women all over the world. Little is known about the origins of this sassy ancient diva, but experts tout one account as the most accurate:

Once upon a time in a small fishing village, a woman lived with her husband, who was captain of a large vessel and commander of an entire fleet of fishing boats. Early on in her marriage, she found out he was cheating on her with a local harlot. In those days, women didn't have any recourse; she kept her mouth shut and hid her knowledge. He never knew she was on to his infidelity, but with each day, she grew more resentful and angry.

One afternoon, her husband went out on the annual week-long fishing expedition with his fleet. Seven days later, when the boats were returning to land, a terrible hurricane hit and destroyed the fleet as well as the houses along the shore. The entire town was flooded and hundreds died, but the captain's wife lived. She huddled in the cold on a large board suspended above the water where their cottage once stood.

When the winds calmed the next morning, she saw a figure in the distance making its way toward her in the water. As it came closer, she saw that it was her husband, and that he was badly injured. He dragged himself along, using all of his strength to get to his wife. When he was close, he yelled out to her, begging her to pull him to safety atop her floating refuge. She grabbed for his hand, but in a moment of vengeance decided instead to say her piece first. She spoke majestically: "All these years I've been telling you I love your seamen," she explained. "You are so cocky, egotistical, and self-centered that you assumed it was a compliment to you. Well, you were wrong. While you were carousing with tramps about town, I was having a lovely time myself with several of the young sailors in your fleet. Those boys are simply divine. I found out early on, my dear, that you are nothing more than a washed-up captain with no control over your seamen." She cackled, turned, and paddled away on the boards that once served as walls of the house that he built. He could hear her laughing as he sank below the surface and took his rightful place along the ocean floor with the moss and scum.

*The best revenge is living well and making sure he knows about it.*

*—Anonymous*

Thus, the goddess of retribution began her quest to help women everywhere take back their lives from the men who wrong them. Today, she's watching over you.

You now have some pointers and creative ideas that can help you look at your relationships in a new way. Life is difficult after a breakup, but the upper hand is yours if you stay sassy and remember how truly fabulous you are. Your reactions, thoughts, and emotions are not crazy or weak in any way. On the contrary, like those of many women who have come before you, they are refreshingly real. Your attitude is a celebration of the spunk and resiliency unique to womankind.

Remember—though it is hard to get over someone you really care about, it is even harder to spend your life in an unfulfilling relationship. Hold out for a person who gives you the love and respect you deserve. In the meantime, the goddess of retribution is watching over you, helping you get through these tough times. Soon you will be able to say, "I used to miss him, but my aim is improving. In fact, now I hit the bull's-eye every time.

# Glossary

**amoeba role:**
A term used to categorize the behavior of a slimy man with no spine.

**bachelorette pad (B-Pad):**
The house or apartment of a single woman with attitude.

**basic battle plan:**
A sassy but mild scheme appropriate for any ex, even those that are merely annoying.

**beauty queen routine:**
A slight variation of standard beauty procedures that works therapeutic post-breakup elements into the mix.

**big crack problem:**
A drug addiction that requires one to eliminate a man from her life immediately; an issue for a man who has an exceedingly large ass.

**bitch flakes:**
A special type of cereal that makes one feel extra sassy.

**breakup club card:**
A mental tally of those good things an ex has done to make up for the horrible things he did during the relationship and breakup; a card which, when completely punched, earns a diva a free latte.

**bullshit meter:**
The natural indicator in one's brain that sends off a signal when a shovel is needed.

**Burberry muzzle**
A contraption fashioned from the signature Burberry print that fits around a friend's face to keep her mouth shut.

**butch lesbian gym teacher:**
An archaic stereotype of the single woman created by intimidated men with no imagination.

**catnip spray:**
A type of cologne given to an ex to wear in the presence of feisty kitties.

**chief executive diva:**
The title of a woman who holds a top position of power in her company; a designation far more flattering than chief executive officer.

**circle of death:**
The tight-knit ring formed by a posse of divas when they're on the social scene; a ring of women impenetrable by other women or men.

**closure spectrum:**
The range indicating how close a diva is to full closure and recovery from a breakup.

**command center:**
A place used to rally support against an ex, usually equipped with a phone, e-mail access, and tissues; the apartment or house of a close male friend when used in this way after a breakup.

**copycat courage:**
A phrase used to refer to any quality or skill acquired from an enemy and then used to overtake him; also known as "copyrat courage" when referring to a particularly obnoxious man.

**Daddy Warbucks look:**
A haircut for men that involves taking off all of the strands to reveal a shiny open surface; sometimes achieved without the assistance of a barber.

**dating diet:**
An approach to the initial phases of dating that treats the guy like a large, flaky pastry or creamy cake to be tasted in moderation.

**déjà vu:**
A relationship with an ex rekindled long after the breakup.

**Delicious Bookstore Babe:**
A fictitious title used as a ploy to get help from a cute guy in a bookstore.

**demolition diva:**
A diva who toys with her ex by doing things that are insolent and playfully bitchy.

**dick mug:**
A personalized mug used for serving coffee, tea, or hot cocoa to any ex.

**discuss the breakup (DTB):**
A mode in which one talks about a breakup nonstop in a compulsive fashion.

**discuss the relationship (DTR):**
A marathon session during which two people talk about their feelings for one another, their time together, and their expectations for the future; a period of talk between two people lasting no less than four hours and usually occurring between midnight and 5 A.M.

**diva:**
A term used to describe any woman with confidence, edge, and enthusiasm.

**divadom:**
The state of being in which one has achieved supreme diva status; the way the world appears to a diva.

**divalicious:**
An adjective used to describe the ultimate, sassy, irresistible woman.

**dynamic diva duo:**
Two women with gumption brought together to avenge one of the women against a man gone bad.

**emotional cocktail:**
The combination of feelings that create a sense of loss after a breakup.

**Ex-Boyfriends-R-Us:**
An ex-boyfriend's place during the time in which a diva is claiming all of his assets as her own.

**exorcise:**
The process of cleansing an ex of the devil inside of him.

**extreme schmuckdom:**
A state in which a man cheats, tells a major lie, or is despicable beyond belief in some other way; calls for an extreme, unforgiving sassy battle plan.

**foremothers:**
Those women upon which the modern world was founded; divas in history who paved the path for sassy women today.

**fugitive glam posse:**
A group of divas fleeing a scary scene full of obnoxious men or horribly geeky stalkers.

**garbage:**
Anything that belongs to an ex.

**glam posse:**
A group of fabulous women assembled to take the social scene by storm.

**Goddess of Retribution:**
A female divinity with no known origin believed to have mystical powers that enable her to fight off man-monsters and vindicate women.

**go-go goddess:**
A diva in a state of perpetual motion and activity.

**Greek goddess Hormonia:**
One of the lesser-known she-gods originating in Athens, Greece, known for her fluctuating emotions and unpredictable fits of rage.

**green gremlin:**
Jealousy that hits after a breakup as a result of real or imagined circumstances; also known as the green-eyed monster.

**himbo:**
A good looking man with no brain; a male bimbo.

**heinous by association:**
Those bars, clubs, or places of any kind that are particularly troublesome because they remind a diva of her ex; an adjective sometimes used to describe an ex's friends.

**Jaguar:**
The male midlife crisis car of choice.

**jail:**
A place to avoid (one cannot get a manicure or pedicure there); an ideal place for an ex to relocate.

**June Cleaver:**
A 1950s sitcom character epitomizing the sassless suburban housewife.

**Let's Be Friends Agreement:**
A pact made in 75 percent of all breakups; secures between the parties sporadic lunches and regular awkward conversation via phone, e-mail, or in person.

**lingering ex:**
A man who just won't go away and continues to perform ambiguous moves until one takes extreme action.

**little white lie:**
A lie told to cover up something positive, e.g., a party, gift, or visitor; a lie of minimal consequence told to avoid major confrontation that would otherwise occur for no good reason.

**lobotomy:**
A procedure commonly performed on boyfriends within the first year of dating.

**lobster diva:**
A woman who has spent too much time in the sun.

**losergator:**
Often substituted into the phrase "See ya later, alligator" when it is said to an ex.

**man stash:**
An assortment of men one is dating simultaneously.

**"me" day:**
A day of relaxation and beauty rituals; a sick day when one is not really sick.

**menacing magic:**
A variation of typical occult practices in which the object is tormented directly, without the intervention of a mythical spirit.

**midget porn:**
A type of program frequently watched by scuzzy men; a show with scintillating dialogue easily remembered by its male viewers.

**mini-breakup:**
one of several smaller breakups that precedes the big finale; a split followed by a short period of reconciliation in which a diva can pull off in-house revenge maneuvers and prepare a sassy battle plan.

**mini-mullet:**
The small strands on the back of a guy's head that grow faster than the rest of his hair; usually serve as first indication that he needs a trim.

**mini-wee:**
An ex's penis; see *wee* and *willy*.

**monsoon season:**
The stage of a relationship in which the breakup is pending.

**motivational crying:**
A type of weeping that inspires one to take action, make life changes, and rise to power.

**ocean floor scum:**
The living creatures an ex most resembles in intelligence and appearance.

**old divas network:**
The group of women in any industry or profession that have gumption and experience; a professional network of women.

**old faithfuls:**
Those items of clothing one wears regularly because they are at the front of the closet.

**pedestal:**
The place a diva sets a boyfriend where she cannot see any of his flaws or issues.

**Perfect Plastic Princess:**
A woman who has plastic surgery every time a tiny flaw appears on her body; a woman who has a face pulled so tight she can't smile without getting a headache.

**perma-smile:**
A grin that never goes away and is obviously fake; a ditsy man or woman's default facial expression; the scary look often made by a nurse, a sorority officer, or a customer service representative.

**pr*ck:**
An uncouth yet appropriate word for describing certain men.

**phone phobia:**
A disease that strikes men and prevents them from calling when they should.

**poison ivy salad:**
A healthy and therapeutic culinary concoction created for an ex.

**Porta Potti:**
A portable loo that's often disgusting and dirty; a temporary bathroom that serves as a surefire indication that a bar should be avoided; an excellent alternative means of disposing of an ex's personal belongings.

**posse fairy godmother:**
A mystical figure that grants a glam posse good fortune on the social scene.

**post-breakup shopping spree:**
A guilt-free day of shopping and selecting stylish, "make him grovel" attire.

**psycho:**
A term used by guilt-ridden men to describe any woman who has shown even the slightest amount of emotion; often a term men use to justify their poor behavior toward a woman.

**public personal space:**
An area in the open where one likes to go alone to people-watch or plot a man's demise.

**purse-free boob job:**
The process by which one's breasts appear larger because money, credit cards, or keys are stuffed in one's bra.

**Queen of Rationalization:**
A woman who can justify any move made by an ex, even one that technically should land him in state prison.

**rebound relief:**
Getting over an ex by finding a new, low-maintenance guy to date right away.

**ruin-his-life cheerleaders:**
Those friends, family members, and acquaintances that form a post-breakup support network for a diva on a mission.

**safety spouse:**
The guy one will marry "in (insert number) years if no one else comes along."

**schmuck lie:**
A lie so big it is completely unforgivable; a lie that moves a guy permanently into the "does not deserve to breathe" category.

**scumbag:**
Any man who lies, cheats, or generally behaves badly.

**selective memory:**
A dubious attribute that allows a diva to remember only the good things about her ex; his bad habits, terrible conversational skills, and nasty behaviors are forgotten quickly, but the one time he put the toilet seat down is remembered for years to come.

**sh*t or get off the pot:**
An age-old expression that means "make a commitment or hit the road."

**Shrinky Dinks:**
A psychiatrist or psychologist who can make even the most depressed diva into an annoyingly happy one; a doctor that shrinks the importance of a breakup in one's mind.

**single moment:**
Any moment in which one feels weird about being single.

**single police:**
Those who ask single people annoying questions like "When are you getting married?"

**singlehood:**
The state of being single.

**situational sass:**
Those gutsy comebacks mustered at the spur of the moment to alleviate a problem or address an irritating situation.

**social hibernation:**
The process of ditching one's glam posse for a boy toy.

**social starlet:**
A celebrity on the social scene.

**sophistabitch:**
A sophisticated bitch, with "bitch" meaning assertive, sassy, and powerful.

**starlet stash:**
Those items at an ex's apartment that belong to the woman.

**Super Bowl Sunday:**
The ideal day to throw a Tupperware party or have a chick-flick marathon at a man's house or apartment.

**super glue lip balm:**
A special type of Chap Stick given only to exes.

**superstar garb:**
The perfect "make him grovel" outfit, purchased during a post-breakup shopping spree.

**superstud:**
A guy who is cute, suave, and appealing in every way.

**Sweet As Pie Act:**
The process of pretending to be naïve to accomplish a goal.

**"take action" attitude:**
A spirited, energetic state in which one does something productive every day.

**That's Impossible Crowd:**
Those people who always have a reason why something will not work.

**the scene:**
A social landscape that includes bars, parties, recreation clubs, outdoor venues, and any other place where people congregate to be social.

**the ultimatum:**
A phrase a man uses to make a woman with good intentions think she has done something wrong by asking where the relationship is going.

**therapeutic travel:**
A trip taken after a breakup, during which one torments her ex from afar.

**tolerably nerdy:**
A geeky guy with redeeming qualities; the perfect man to give any diva a post-breakup ego boost; a guy that often grows into a stud worth marrying.

**tourniquet dress:**
A dress so tight one's circulation is cut off.

**Viagra spam:**
An indication that one's e-mail is working.

**vixen:**
A role a diva plays when she's dressed to the nines and feels fun and flirtatious.

**wedding hawk:**
A person who will not stop asking one questions about one's plans for marriage; usually a mother, a married sibling, or a married friend.

**wee**
A more couth word to say in public when referring to a man's penis; originating amongst children and therefore having a

demeaning quality when used in reference to an adult male's anatomy; also referred to as a willy.

**willy:**
See *wee*.

**wing women:**
Those friends who are by one's side out on the scene; see *glam posse*.

**worthy:**
An adjective commonly used to describe a man who deserves more than one date.

## About the Author

ALISON JAMES is a coffee shop therapist for New York City's most confident singletons. She is an expert in the breakup field, with more than two decades of experience using the recovery plan she reveals in this book. She lives in New York City.